110659033

A Passion for the Glory:
The Architectural Framework of
Prophetic Ministry and Imagination

A Passion for the Glory:
The Architectural Framework
of Prophetic Ministry and Imagination
by
Dr. Mark J. Chironna

Vincom Publishing Company
Tulsa, Oklahoma

Unless otherwise indicated, all Scripture quotations are taken from the *King James Version of the Bible*. Other quotes are from *The Holy Bible, New Revised Standard Version*, (New York-Oxford: Oxford University Press, copyright © 1989 by the Division of Christian Education of the National Council of the Churches of Christ in the United States; illustrations copyright © 1990 by Doubleday Book & Music Clubs, Inc.

A Passion for the Glory:
The Architectural Framework
of Prophetic Ministry and Imagination
ISBN 0-927936-95-X
Copyright © 1996 by
Mark J. Chironna
Higher Call Cosmopolitan Church
7001 Old Wake Forest Road
Raleigh, NC 27604

Published by VINCOM PUBLISHING CO.
P. O. Box 702160
Tulsa, OK 74170
(918) 254-1276

Printed in the United States of America.
All rights reserved under International Copyright Law.
Contents and/or cover may not be reproduced in whole or in part in any form without the express written consent of the Publisher.

Dedication

To my two sons, Matthew and Daniel, who represent my hope for the future.

Contents

Foreword

First, allow me to thank my good friend Mark Chironna for allowing me to write the Foreword for this great book, which has truly blessed me in my personal reading and devotional time.

Mark has a very special prophetic gift that is both oral and written. In this book, you will sense the prophetic voice of God in written form.

In the Bible, we find John the Baptist was called to be a voice in the wilderness. While reading this book, God spoke to me about how prophetic this book is for our wilderness world that is calling for a voice.

The wilderness represents a place that is a wasteland, a desert, a place of drought, a place of unproductiveness, a place that lacks hope, vision, and dreams. Does this not sound like our world today? The world is calling for such a prophetic voice that will come in and prepare the way for Christ to come in the power of the Holy Spirit and do the miraculous, which brings forth healing, conviction, and prosperity in the lives of people today.

I believe Mark is one of the very few chosen of God to speak His prophetic voice in the wilderness (our world). He is a true man with the prophetic gift of insight and interpretation. He speaks the revelation knowledge of God, which opens up the heavens and sends down the rain that heals this wilderness land.

I thank God for knowing such a prophet, who is not afraid to write the prophetic word of God into layman's language so that the youngest ears of the Body of Christ might understand the truthfulness of who they are in Christ, and that they may act upon God's power and fulfill the purpose to which they have been called.

In Jeremiah 37:17, King Zedekiah asked Jeremiah the Prophet, "Is there any word from the Lord?" This is the question the wilderness world is asking today in the midst of local, national, and global corruption. This is the question the world is asking in the midst of drug-infested communities, teenage pregnancies, single-parent homes, and over-populated prisons.

Where are those prophets today who can answer this question? We have found a prophet who can answer this question, and the answer is in this book.

This book is must-reading for every pastor, teacher, minister, and Christian. It will assist you in your global knowledge and daily walk with Christ, so that you may be more effective in your testimony of who Christ is.

Finally, this book will help you to become more intimately acquainted with the voice of God and charge you to be obedient.

God bless you, Mark, for being an inspired, chosen vessel to speak life into a dying world. I love you.

— Bishop Eddie L. Long

Introduction

Every person has a worldview, known or unknown. . . an attitude toward life, a certain perception of reality [a paradigm] . . . A worldview is really a kind of Theory of Everything (TOE), a comprehensive vision that plausibly explains all that is to the satisfaction of those who hold it.[1]

— Howard A. Snyder

The time has come for the Church to reconsider her understanding of the place and purpose of prophetic directives and the call of God upon men and women with a prophetic mandate.

Professor and author Howard A. Snyder in his biblically based book of megatrends in world change, sees major disruptions in societies and cultures coming as we live through the times leading to the "new world order" of Jesus, opposed by the forces of darkness attempting to set up their new world order.

We face a great season of transition and a paradigm shift in the world at large — perhaps the greatest since the crucifixion and resurrection of Christ. In this time of crisis, it behooves us to look again with new eyes at the role the prophetic voice plays in the arena of life.

The word *paradigm* is being used extensively today in fields that are wide and varied. It comes from the Greek *paradigma,* and means "model" or "pattern," a collection of thoughts or ideas that make up the way one sees life. A "paradigm shift" is like an earthquake in one's life or in society as a whole.

In this book, I attempt to show that no such world shifts affecting God's people have occurred *without* His voice being heard in warnings and/or promises through His prophets. No changes in earth's history have occurred without God speaking forth a creative word through His prophets to forward His plan and purpose.

The upheaval of society at every level from the family to the global marketplace — and everything in between — is, I believe, merely "the beginning of birthpangs." (Matthew 24:8 NRSV) Everything indicates that a new era is about to break upon us.

If ever there was a time in history when a multitude of voices were attempting to get our attention, it is now. However, it is not "voices" we need to hear, but rather the *one true voice*. If God indeed is speaking, then He must be about His one and only purpose. Therefore, we must recover the sense of what He is about and align ourselves with that intention.

However, we cannot know what He is about apart from His existential word to this generation:

• There must be those who have been groomed and prepared to lift up the sacred text of Holy Writ once again.

• There must be those trained and prepared to recover the very sense of the present, powerful, invasive, intruding Word which speaks order to the chaos left by the 20th century "storms" and meaning to the void left in our lives.

1
The Need for Recovery and Restoration

> Slowly I realized that *my worldview had changed in a moment, in the twinkling of an eye.* By faith, I had plunged my hand through the metallic fabrication of Western intellect and laid hold of something real. I could no longer accept teachings that flowed out of the brass heaven.[1]
>
> — Douglas McMurry

Our day is not unlike a time when the "prophets" of the royal court were falsely reassuring Zedekiah that all would be well, while the voice of the true prophet (Jeremiah) was sinking in the mud of an empty cistern at the brink of death. They were manufacturing "words" from *a brass heaven,* while Jeremiah was speaking forth the true Word of God.

However, at the darkest moment of night when all should be at rest, the king, who had appeared to have everything under control in the midst of upheaval, was instead restless and *out of control.*

His soothsayers had not spoken to the reality of what he sensed deep in his spirit. He was impelled, in a moment of secrecy, to come to Jeremiah, whom he previously had attempted to silence. Indeed this has always been the tendency amongst those who refuse to hear: Silence the prophets!

Therefore, the king, perhaps rather sheepishly, made a request of the prophet: **Is there any word from the Lord?** (Jeremiah 37:17).

1

Those steeped in the status quo have a difficult time embracing the dynamic of change. Yet God is not static; therefore the *status quo* is a place He can neither remain nor endure. It was Jeremiah, not the king and his courtiers nor even the religious leaders, who understood God in the extremity of the condition in which Judah was embroiled.

Jeremiah was most concerned with what was going on behind the scenes in the heavenly arena. This chained, humiliated, weeping-over-sins prophet had the key to bring the nation through transition. He had the existential *word* for the hour.

Jeremiah understood that the Jerusalem which Judah had known for centuries was about to come to an end. He also understood how that change was going to be brought about.

Human Nature Resists Change

Something new was breaking in upon the old world of Jerusalem, something new which those of Judah refused to accept and embrace or even understand. They reacted just as had their brothers and sisters in the northern nation of Israel, who had failed to embrace repentance and change some 120 years before. The end of those ten tribes had been exile to Assyria.

In the context of the threat to Judah from the empire of Babylon, God allowed their "world" to undergo great upheaval and cataclysmic chaos. However, the Royal Court prophets were committed to maintaining the old world as they had known it.

Once "status quo" establishes its parameters, it endeavors to *manage* God rather than *follow* God. It parades itself as God's representative, while in actual fact, it seeks to effectively silence God in the mud of a waterless dungeon or cistern.

Jeremiah perceived the end and wept, while his fellow Israelites were blinded and could not grieve. They had lost the ability to feel the pain and pathos of God *or* His glory, which had all but vanished from view. Public opinion polls have no validity with God, whose Kingdom is *not* a democracy.

It requires the ending of an old world for a new world to begin, and the process of grief for sin is an essential element in the shaping of people for a new thing. The groaning of created things is what frees mature sons from futility. (Romans 8:18-22.) The radicality of "hope not seen" empowers the visionary to travail in grief until the old thing dies and the new arises.

The prophetic word and voice must be recovered if we are to be able to deal effectively with the destination of the Church in our time. The WORD of the Lord creates *ex nihilo* (out of nothing), and there can be no new thing unless we hear that Word.

> **Surely the Lord God will do nothing, but he revealeth his secret unto his servants the prophets.**
>
> **Amos 3:7**

We must find where the WORD of the Lord has been imprisoned in the castles of man-made kingdoms and recover it, lest it be silenced in the oblivion of the pit. That is where the forces of darkness seek to prevent its being heard. (Psalm 103:4.) It is the recovery of that WORD *in the mouth of the prophet* that will release the power of God into the social structure of the Church and society and eventually restructure nations until they bear the image of His glory.

In Peter.s address to the crowd who witnessed the healing of the lame man at the Beautiful Gate, he stated in clear and powerful language his understanding and insight into the very purpose of God as revealed by the voices of the prophets of old. He declared:

> **But those things, which God before had shewed by the mouth of all his prophets, that Christ should suffer, he hath so fulfilled.**

Repent ye therefore, and be converted, that your sins may be blotted out, when the times of refreshing shall come from the presence of the Lord;

And he shall send Jesus Christ, which before was preached unto you:

Whom the heaven must receive until the times of restitution of all things, which God hath spoken by the mouth of all his holy prophets since the world began.

For Moses truly said unto the fathers, A prophet shall the Lord your God raise up unto you of your brethren, like unto me; him shall ye hear in all things whatsoever he shall say unto you.

And it shall come to pass, that every soul, which will not hear that prophet, shall be destroyed from among the people.

Yea, and all the prophets from Samuel and those that follow after, as many as have spoken, have likewise foretold of these days.

Ye are the children (sons) of the prophets, and of the covenant which God made with our fathers, saying unto Abraham, And in thy seed shall all the kindreds of the earth be blessed.

Acts 3:18-25

There is a clear progression revealed in those verses that begins with repentance (*metanoia*), a turning to God as a result of a change in the mind. In other words, the "old world," which the citizens of Judah thought would never change, had changed. The word of the Lord came through Jeremiah that the culture and society in which they lived had come to an end.

Survival Means Embracing God's Changes

God said they needed to embrace transition and change their "worldview." His original word to them of "hear and obey" (Deuteronomy 6:3), meant they were to embrace the "new" thing He was doing as a result of their disobedience. He had a new *paradigm* for them.

> Yet they obeyed not, nor inclined their ear, but walked every one in the imagination of their evil heart: therefore I will bring upon them all the words of this covenant, which I commanded them to do; but they did them not.
>
> And the Lord said unto me, A conspiracy is found among the men of Judah, and among the inhabitants of Jerusalem.
>
> They are turned back to the iniquities of their forefathers . . . .
>
> Jeremiah 11:8-10

Repentance, or turning again, leads to a season of refreshing. Times and seasons of repentance water the dry soil of limited perception and narrow-minded thinking. The "ground" of a hardened heart is softened to receive a new planting of the Seed, Christ, Who can transform chaos into a new order.

The Man in the glory has already been appointed for what is taking place today. The refreshing comes from Him, goes through Him, and will ultimately return to Him. (Romans 11:36.) He is both Lord and Christ. His presence with the Church is for a time not manifest in bodily form, but He has come in the power of His Spirit, His anointing, to bring about the necessary changes.

The Man in the glory will remain in the glory of the heavenly tabernacle and occupy that place, even as He was lifted into that arena at the ascension. However, in the seasons and era of the Church militant, the spirit of Elijah (Malachi 4:5,6) is operational as a spirit of restoration and recovery both in the moral and the spiritual fiber of the Church.

This Spirit was manifest in the person of John the Baptist as a preparatory anointing for the arrival of

Messiah, the biggest paradigm shift of all history. Jesus Himself alluded to the matter of restoration and recovery inherent in the spirit of Elijah. (Matthew 17:11.)

The primary issue to us, therefore, ought to be this matter of *recovery and restoration*. If we truly understand the purpose and manner of the prophetic ministry and imagination, we will realize that those in prophetic ministry can discern the season in which we live and speak the "new thing" prior to its arrival.

This, in essence, is *the purpose of the prophetic voice*:

It involves the dismantling of the "old" thing that has outlived its usefulness and the calling forth of the radically "new" thing that is about to arrive.

In fact, the "new" thing is really God's original intention, which has been completed from eternity past. At these times of transition when a portion of His completed intention comes into natural view, He is actually declaring the end from the beginning. (Isaiah 46:10; Acts 15:18.)

The prophetic call takes us "back to the future" (to borrow a phrase from Hollywood). Restoration implies the state and act of something being returned to its original, former, normal, unimpaired condition. It brings the original back to its soundness, health, and vigor.[2]

Times of refreshing, however, are not synchronous with the epochs or periods of restoration, but rather are *preparatory* to those periods.

For Jeremiah, it was the creative and intrusive speech of Yahweh in his mouth that first dismantled ("plucked up, broke down, destroyed and overthrew"). Then the Word would have restored ("build and plant") — if the Israelites had received and allowed it to restore them to right fellowship with their covenant God. (Jeremiah 1:10.)

There was something lost and in need of recovery, and the prophet saw the unseen hand of the Almighty at work to bring a transition to His people. Thus, Jeremiah began to address the upheaval as the breaking-in of God with newness yearned for but not expressed. The prophet expressed in speech the buried longings and repressed fears of a people who must have a "word from the Lord" in order to live and survive.

Prophets Tell of God's Intentions

Old Testament prophets provide for us an architectural framework from which to reshape the imagination of a contemporary people. The Church today, God's people, must comprehend the basic elemental changes taking place at the very foundations of society and speak to them with the power to create newness out of the fallen debris.

The prophet sees the intention of God and stands outside the paradigm of "the way we've always done it around here." This kind of ministry is characterized by a fresh and original revelation of Christ and the Father's purpose in Christ from eternity to eternity. The prophet can only speak what she or he sees, which is a heavenly, not earthly, reality. This so grips the imagination of their souls that it causes them to call the Church to radical spirituality and demand a departure from corrupt religiosity.

The consuming passion of the prophet is indeed the glory of God to fill the earth. (Psalm 72:19.) The progressive revelation of Christ is the core of what all true prophets can see or hear. If there is no relationship in events and current thinking to Christ the Head and Christ the Body, they find no purpose in things whatsoever. They see the absolute Headship of Christ and the sovereign rule of Christ in the Body by the power of the Spirit.

For these fresh voices, there can be no middle ground. Everything is holy ground. They are consumed with the fire of God and energized by the remembrance of His goings in former days. They are radicalized by hopes of a future yet to be that He has let them see, although those hopes, long deferred, have at times made their hearts heavy.

(Proverbs 13:12.)

Whether it is Jeremiah in days of sorrow, Elijah in the cave of depressive vulnerability, or Jonah in a season of frustration and absolute despair, these are the voices that call us to newness. (Jeremiah 15:18; 1 Kings 19:9; Jonah 4:9, respectively.) True prophets see the glory and purpose of God, cannot rest where others are comfortable, and are after the recovery of something in the earth which they know is missing.

Christians, in general, tend to want to silence these voices, because they cause consternation among us. (Ezekiel 3:15.) It is easier to remain in "what is" rather than embrace what could be. There is a certain security, howbeit false, that lulls and dulls us into complacent indifference to the forward momentum of God's goings. We prefer the ease of complacency to the agitation of destiny.

This intrusive voice that shatters our presuppositions and calls us to embrace the radicality of what we might not be able to see, although prophets tell us it exists, is too costly for us. We must leave the world as we have known it, if we are to embrace God's world as He has declared it to be from before the foundations of the earth.

The Church has become locked in and "enculturated" by the ways of society. We have "walked in the counsel of the godless" (Psalm 1:1), for we thought we could partner with darkness in order to convert it. However, we are beginning to discover that once we walk in that counsel, we stand in the same path as the sinner. Thus, we find ourselves in the company of those who scoff at the possibility of life beyond the desert sands of Babylon.

Bible scholars tell us that Psalm 1 was written during the time of Jeremiah, when the majority of those living in Judah had failed to heed the Word of the Lord. All they could "hear" was the oncoming bitter captivity. Rather than repent for idolatry and refusal to hear God, they blamed Jeremiah. They accused him of being in "cahoots" with the

Babylonians, when he told them captivity was God's present will for them. (Jeremiah 37:13.)

The Way of Death Is To "Kill" the Prophets

The "way of life" for them was to accept the *paradigm* shift and return to the Lord and His ways *in* Babylon. The prophet had explained that, if they turned back to Him, God would bless them in exile. (Jeremiah 21:9, 29:4-15.) The "way of death" was to try to remain in Judah, go to Egypt, or merge with Babylon. (Jeremiah 29:9.)

Sad to say, because of the hardness of heart of the majority of Jeremiah's countrymen, once in Babylon, most did become "enculturated" into a Babylonian paradigm. They continued to refuse the paradigm of God as revealed in His words through His prophet. The few who did see became "a remnant of a remnant," so to speak (Judah already was "the remnant of Israel" — Jeremiah 6:9).

This idea of a "pure remnant" of God's people, cleansed in fiery trial so that they became perfectly submitted and obedient to God's purpose, is one of the most prominent themes in Isaiah. (Isaiah 4:2-4, 10:20-22, 37:30-32.) There always will be a remnant in any age that remains true to God.

The "remnant" were those who heard Jeremiah clearly enough to know that, even if they had to go to Babylon, they would see a recovery of the promise and a restoration of the temple after 70 years. (Jeremiah 25:12, 29:4-15.) These, like Ezekiel and Daniel, found themselves by "rivers of living water" in the desert.

They did not walk, or stand, or eventually sit enthroned in the place of mockery. Rather, they became transplanted trees thriving like "roots out of parched ground" (Isaiah 53:2), because they embraced the radical word that promised newness. They refused to be shaped by the dominant culture in which they lived. They were "in the world but not of the world." (John 15:19.)

As a result they became the embodiment of a hope yet realized and an expression of the intention of God yet to manifest. They became the testimony of what God would do in the days that lay ahead of them. They bore fruit in the fruitless place. Firmly planted in the most unlikely soil, they were nourished by a stream of life that found its way to them.

I am using these historical events, of course, as metaphors and pictures of God's intention and desire for the Church. These things cannot be or come to be, unless we embrace the need for recovery and restoration. Both are tied to the Word of the Lord in the mouth of the prophets.

Walter Breuggemann made a profound and timely statement when he wrote:

> The task of prophetic ministry is to nurture, nourish, and evoke a consciousness and perception alternative to the consciousness and perception of the dominant culture around us.[3]

The vision of what ought to be is held in the imagination of the prophet, countering the sight of what is. Present reality does not undermine the prophetic vision, but provides the creative tension necessary to release God's vision.

Prophetic speech is faith-filled and history-making. It can reshape the discrepancy of present-day reality, even as a potter refashions formless clay on a wheel. (Jeremiah 18:1-6.) Prophetic words, when truly "heard" with the spirit, allow God to make us into vessels of the future fit to bear the glory of His dream, which has been forgotten by us. (Romans 9:21.) At His reshaping, we awaken to remember His dream.

2

The Voice That Cries in the Wilderness

> For when prophetic vision penetrates the thick darkness, the cloud is seen to be alive with winged creatures, with cherubim and seraphim. The sound of its coming is, in the prophetic idiom, the sound of their wings.[1] (Ezekiel 1:24.)
>
> — Meredith Kline

The shaping of the vessel that bears the *imago Dei* is done in remote places, for God has chosen to fashion in unlikely soil those who bear the glory. The Lord does nothing in vain and does all things well. He is ever guided by His unchangeable purpose. From the very outset of events, we can catch glimpses of truth until they unfold into the full flower of divine revelation as to His intention.

It is easier to answer David's question, when he asks, **What is man, that thou art mindful of him?** (Psalm 8:4), than it is to answer the question, "What is the image of God in man"?

Scripture reveals that God indeed chose to make man in His image and in His likeness. (Genesis 1:26.) What that means and how that is fashioned is not as readily discernible as some might think. If we understand how God takes a man, leads him into a desert place, reshapes and fashions him into something after His heart, then commands that man to lift his voice in the wilderness, we can begin to comprehend the image of God.

I am indebted to the work of Meredith Kline who has helped shape and form my understanding of the image of the glory of God in the face of Christ. Kline's contention is that we must rediscover the glory cloud in the very beginning of God's activity in creation if we hope to understand the shaping and molding of man into His image and glory.[2]

We are told that, in the beginning, God created the heavens and the earth, and that the earth was in a state of utter judgment and ruin. (Genesis 1:2.) The Hebrew words translated "without form and void" are used by the prophets to describe ruination and waste. Jeremiah used the same phrase to cry out regarding judgment:

> **I beheld the earth, and, lo, it was without form, and void; and the heavens, and they had no light.**
>
> **Jeremiah 4:23**

Isaiah used the same phrase to describe land after times of judgment:

> **But the cormorant** (pelican) **and the bittern** (porcupine or hedgehog) **shall possess it; the owl also and the raven shall dwell in it: and he shall stretch out upon it the *line of confusion*** (desolation), **and the stones** (plumbline) **of emptiness.**
>
> **Isaiah 34:11**

To be without form is to be a "waste howling wilderness," according to the words of Moses. (Deuteronomy 32:10.) The Hebrew words *tohu* and *bohu* of Genesis 1:2 ("without form and void") are the "waste howling wilderness" of Moses. What we have in these verses is a clear and precise insight and revelation of the nature of God and His activity in the earthly arena.

We are told that in the days of creation, the wind or breath of God (*ruach*) was "brooding" over the face of the waters. (Genesis 1:2.) Even this word *brood* has tremendous import in regards to the prophetic glory God releases when His image is seen. The breath, or wind, of God brooded over the chaos.

This Hebrew word describes an eagle brooding over her young. It is used by Moses in that sense to portray Yahweh in metaphorical terms as a mother eagle hovering over her young and bringing them to a place of true maturity. (Exodus 19:4.) As a mother spreads out her wings to guide her young, so the Lord spreads out His wings in the glory to overshadow His young and bring them into full stature.

An announcement was made at the beginning of the story of creation that God created the "heaven and the earth." (Genesis 1:1.) Then there was an apparent disruption, as the earth became "formless and void." Apparently, there was a partial ruination of what God created.[3] However, immediately, there is His Presence, His brooding Spirit, in actual fact — His Glory, hovering over the desolation to restore and recover.

God Never Gives Up His Plans

God began then, in the clear and careful sequence related in Genesis 1, to re-establish a framework in which, by the end of the sixth day, He was prepared to place His image in the earth. When His image is seen, His intention is to rest there. In Kline's words:

> It was actually by means of His glory-presence that God thus led His people at the time of the exodus. It was in the pillar of cloud and fire that He went before the Israelites on the way from Egypt to the promised land and afforded them overshadowing protection. To describe the action of the glory cloud by the figure of outstretched wings was natural, not simply because of the overshadowing function it performed, but because of the composition of this theophanic cloud. . . .
>
> Reflecting on Genesis 1:2, Psalm 104 envisages the Creator Spirit as the One Who makes the clouds His chariot and moves on the wings of the wind, making the winds His angel-messengers

and flames His servants. When we recognize this theophanic cloud-and-wind form of the Spirit in Genesis 1:2, the literary connection between the original creation record and certain redemptive recreation narratives becomes more luminous.[4]

This "voice" that cries in the desolate place, in the wilderness, as depicted in Isaiah 40:3, is the thunderous voice of the glory cloud ushered in on the wings of the wind.

• It is this voice (*qol*, in the Hebrew) which is the voice of the Lord.

• It is this voice which has the ability to restructure the world (Genesis 1:2) and also frighten fallen man (Genesis 3:8), as the cloud approaches announcing His arriving presence.

• It is this voice that agitated and shook Mount Sinai. (Exodus 19:19.)

• It is this voice that thunders over the waters, is powerful, majestic, splits the cedars of Lebanon, hews out flames of fire, shakes the wilderness, makes the deer to give birth, and strips the forest bare, according to the psalmist. (Psalm 29.)

• It is this voice incorrectly translated "still" and "small" in 1 Kings 19:12, *The King James Version* of the Bible. There was indeed a distinct difference between the sound of the earthquake, the fire, and the voice. However, the voice (*qol*) was far from still and small. Elijah was reintroduced afresh to the sound of the glory cloud approaching on the wings of the Spirit.

• It is this voice that shapes the prophets.

• It is this voice that defines the prophetic calling.

• It is indeed this voice that beckons all who "have ears to hear" (Deuteronomy 29:4) to follow the cloud wherever it may lead.

In order to hear this voice, all other voices must effectively be silenced for a season. For this reason, every prophetic voice from the beginning to the end of Scripture was called to a desert or wilderness place for a season to be shaped by a voice not contained in the systems of man's making.

The voice of the Lord is heard in the context of the restorative purpose of God. Therefore, wherever we find desolation and waste, chaos and upheaval, somewhere above is divine wisdom at work to reconfigure the seeming morass of confusion and to bring all things to a new place.

The field of quantum physics has now embraced a science of "chaology." George Land, scientist turned motivational business educator, describes how every system in nature goes through a process of change (chaos) leading to renewal and transformation. He had related his studies in quantum fields to the structures of society in terms of our institutions, coming to the conclusion that the same "laws" operate as in physics.[5]

He labeled it "the Theory of Transformation." Land's observations in all fields of science, including biology, chemistry, atomic physics, and cosmology, led him to draw startling conclusions. However, his conclusions only affirm biblical patterns which lead to powerful breakthroughs and changes that are nothing less than amazing.

What Land would call in scientific terms "a breakpoint phase," we would call theologically and prophetically *an exodus event*. This is a place where God makes "a way out of no way," and ushers in something new that never existed before, at least in that form. The forces of change inherent in the cloud of glory are seen over and over by those apprehended by the Spirit.

God's Movements Are Signposts

These movements of God provide for the prophetic individual an architectural framework, a model, a paradigm, through which the future can be discerned and even realized, if the rules are adhered to that govern the changes. The prophetic voice must find the ancient and well-worn path that others have trod and discover in the process the voice crying in the wilderness of desolation.

There the person under a prophetic call must have an encounter with the knowledge of the holy and experience the *numinous* to be transformed, never to be the same once they return from their time of seclusion. I want to make a significant point here that I feel is essential:

The Church has yet to fully comprehend the foundational truth of apostolic and prophetic ministry.

Paul tells us plainly that the Church is built upon the foundation of the apostles and the prophets, and that Christ Jesus is the Cornerstone. (Ephesians 2:20.) Scripture makes it very clear that, whatever these giftings are presumed to have been in the past, they did not cease after the ascension. Instead, they have their very genesis in the exaltation of Christ.

Each of us has a "Jerusalem" where we were enculturated. As a result, our paradigms (ways of viewing ourselves and the world) were set for us before we knew what they were. Therefore, many Christians have been "programmed" with the doctrine that these gifts are not for today. Many have fought the Spirit of God on this issue to the point where they are "imprisoning truth" in a waterless dungeon as happened to Jeremiah. (Jeremiah 37:16, 38:9-13.)

Both the apostolic and the prophetic gift are essential to the work of God in the Church. To consign them to an earlier age is to ignore the very clear frame of reference from which Paul speaks in Ephesians and thus to be guilty of *reductionism* (reducing "the big picture" to a small doctrine, or event). In many ways, we have been "domesticated" (a bringing under authority by imposition of a stronger force) to an incomplete paradigm that has stolen a portion of the soul of the Church.

The functional qualifications of apostolic and prophetic ministry are woven into the seamless garment of the Lord's glory which He seeks to invest in the Body He is preparing. (Exodus 39:22-26; John 19:23.) These are foundational to the very structure of any local church, if that local expression is to be a "whole" and complete prototype of the larger and greater Body of Christ.

The true Church has no denominational walls and indeed is found in every denomination. Her heart is for the wholeness of Christ, and like Rachel, she weeps for her children. (Matthew 2:18)

The tendency towards reducing Scripture to fit an incomplete model of what God intended causes the "royal court" (those who fear the birth of the true King) to avoid the end of their domain. Thus, there always is an attempt by the "established religious order" to obliterate any and all "new" expressions of the Kingdom before they have a chance to mature. (Matthew 2:16-18.)

In my book, *The Undiscovered Christ*, I dealt with the metaphor of Rachel weeping for her children at length.[6] (I would encourage the reader to obtain a copy for further discussion of the issue of travail and grief in regards to the destruction of the forces of chaos that masquerade as order.)

It behooves us to look again at the context in which Paul places these ascension gifts. We must realize there was indeed a breakpoint and a change that took place at the ascension. The true paradigm shifted in favor of the "new thing" the Lord of Hosts was doing, *which includes ascension gifts.*

The issue of a pattern to follow is so essential to the writers of Scripture that to miss the pattern is to break the rules. To violate the pattern is to suffer the loss of the glory. Consider the numerous texts of Scripture about the importance of a pattern being established and its foundational importance: Exodus 25:9,40; Numbers 8:4; Joshua 22:2?

2 Kings 16:10; 1 Chronicles 28:11-19; Ezekiel 43:10; 1 Timothy 1:16; Hebrews 8:5. (In Hebrews 8:5, the text reveals the "pattern" in a *Man*, which will be discussed at length in Chapter 3.)

In all of the scriptures listed, there are direct admonitions by God or by those in places of leadership to regard carefully the model, pattern, or paradigm being revealed. If Moses had not built the tabernacle and its furnishings in compliance with the pattern given him on the mountain, he would have forfeited the glory descending to abide on the structure.

Whether it be the tabernacle or the temple, or the life of Christ as He arose out of the watery chaos of the Jordan, there is a cloud of glory that descends and rests on a model, a paradigm, a pattern. (Exodus 40:34; 2 Chronicles 5:11-14; Luke 3:21,22.)

Jesus Is the Image, Our Model

Jesus is the very Tabernacle of God, now fleshed out and incarnated, upon which the glory will rest and abide. (John 1:14.) He is the paradigm, the model, the Son whom God will display as His ultimate intention. It is conformity to this image that God is working to bring about. Paul referred to this truth when he clearly stated that Christ Jesus intended to show forth a pattern in him. (1 Timothy 1:16.)

It is not the focus of this book to argue with those who reject the model of the ascension-gift ministries for today or to prove the validity of the operation of all five in the Church. (Ephesians 4:11-15.) However, it is the conviction of the author that the gifts have been and will ever be operational in the Church until the Second Advent. I believe those who have "ears to hear" recognize the clarity of Scripture in this matter.

If our paradigm is different than that of Scripture, there can be no glory made manifest in the corporate structure. Apostolic and prophetic gifts to the Church are for the foundational purpose of *seeing the pattern, and then build-ing* according to the pattern that has been seen.

In this book, we will carefully look at models of prophetic ministry to help us grasp the intention of God in the work He is about in His Church. I refer once again to Meredith Kline:

> The Spirit of God hovered over the primeval tohu not only as a creating power but as a *paradigm* for creation. The theophanic glory was an archetypal pattern for the cosmos and for man, *the image of God*. In order to perceive this archetypal working of the Spirit and appreciate its significance for the image-of-God idea, we must have a fairly distinct apprehension of the Bible's representation of the multifaceted phenomenon of the glory-Spirit that was present at the creation.[7]

The chaotic and watery atmosphere of the earth in Genesis 1:2 was being hovered over by the brooding presence of the glory cloud. In the context of heaven's glory brooding over the chaotic and watery wilderness of judgment and ruin, a *voice* cried out in ten distinct fiats, "Let there be" — and there was.

This voice from the throne was the creative and recre-ative voice of God Himself, endeavoring to recover and restore His original intention and redeem His paradigm in the earth. He then set about building another "temple," this time from the dust (Genesis 2:7), fashioning it in such a way that it would bear the image of the glory in a more personal and intimate way.

To grasp this at the very outset of reading and study-ing the Bible is to be able to follow the thought and intent of God until we come to the consummation of His purpose, in which there is a Temple-City where the glory will abide forever. (Revelation 21.)

The prophets of old spoke continually of restoration and recovery of that image and intention. They peered through the lens of that intention and saw down the corridors of time to a day when God's heart and purpose would be realized in man. When "in the fulness of time" (Galatians 4:4) God sent His Son, the image in the glory cloud that cast a shadow under the old covenant could clearly be seen.

It formed a "cross-like" tabernacle and temple. Each piece of furniture was sprinkled with the blood of a lamb. Each piece correlated with the place of Christ's wounds at the cross. The hinder-parts of His glory (Exodus 33:23), were a shadow of the face and image of Christ. In former times, the object standing in the unapproachable and ineffable light of glory cast a shadow so immense that Moses saw the purpose of God in the image of Christ from the backside of the cross.

The prophetic vision of Moses was of the image of God in Christ. He saw the altar of burnt offering as the place of entry and the gate at which we approach God. At the foot of the cross, the blood flowed from the spike in His feet, the meeting place of God and man. We are bought with a price (1 Corinthians 7:23) and come in abject poverty of spirit (Isaiah 64:6) to be received into the fullness of Him Who is our Head. (Ephesians 4:13.)

We can see that every place in the Old Covenant tabernacle and temple, from the altar to the holy of holies, corresponds to the ascending grace of God. The "types" in the tabernacle/temple extend from the foot of the cross to the bleeding side of Christ, from where water and blood flowed to wash us. (John 19:34.)

Following this pattern enables us to enter into the inner court where we have the light of the Word, the bread of His presence, and the crushed heart of worship at the altar of incense. By death to our flesh, we pass through that veil into the heights of His glory. The crown of thorns provided the blood of sprinkling on the very throne/mercy-seat where we reign with Him as a result of having the mind of Christ by virtue of His finished work.[8] (1 Corinthians 2:16.)

The shadow gave way to the substance of Christ at Golgatha. But the men of old saw more than a death and a burial, they saw a resurrection and an ascension, to the end that God might fill the earth with His glory-image. (Numbers 14:21; Psalm 22:27, 72:19, 102:16; Isaiah 6:3, 59:19, 66:18; Habakkuk 2:14; Zechariah 14:9.)

There was indeed a "breakpoint" change that occurred at Calvary, when "new things" began. The ascension marked the beginning of the release of giftings in the earth, not the cessation of them. The apostolic and prophetic voices in the earth are calling Christians to see the wilderness of their lives and then to see society transformed by the power and the image of the glory of God in the face of Christ.

Foundational ministries (Ephesians 2:20) see an image, even as Isaiah saw an image (Isaiah 6:1), a Man on the throne. As Isaiah was overwhelmed by the vision of God and delivered from partial spiritual blindness and sensory deprivation, these voices crying in the wilderness of contemporary society have "seen" the light of an image. Once that image is seen, they cannot un-see it!

The revelation of the vision of the image of glory is so all-consuming it fills their field of vision. Even as the train of His robe filled the temple in Isaiah's day, so the vision of the reign of the image/Son of God fills them.

They speak of that image and call the Church prophetically to be shaped and built into it. They are endeavoring to cooperate with the Spirit until that image fills the corporate "new thing," the temple made of "living stones." (1 Peter 2:5.) Christ *is* the fullness (fulfillment) of all things. (Ephesians 1:23; Colossians 1:19.)

The giving of the gifts of the ascension is clearly tied in Paul's thinking as expressed in Ephesians to the intention God has to fill all things in Christ. His absolute victory over the forces of chaos and depravity were a result of His humiliation, even to the point of the deepest descent. (Ephesians 4:8-10.)

His humiliation was for the express intention of ascension far above the highest of the heavens, surpassing even the Hebrew notion of the multiplicity of heavens, into the very heights of glory. (Hebrews 12:2.) The giving of these ascension gifts from the sublime glory was so that His glory might be poured out on everyone who is the recipient of His grace, until **every eye shall see him** (Revelation 1:7).

3

The Testimony of the Man

His divine message, given out of the whirlwind, occupies 123 verses (in Job), yet there is not a word about the sufferings of Job, or even about human suffering in general. What God does talk about is creation! ... This leads us to the remarkable conclusion that a correct and complete doctrine of creation is the answer to all (our) problems ....[1]

— Henry M. Morris

What Genesis 1:2 identifies as Spirit, Hebrews 1:2,3 identifies as Son: *God is One.* Hebrews 1:2b attributes to the Son the creation of the world. Then, before the sustaining, directing role of the Son in divine providence is dealt with in Hebrews 1:3b, He is identified as the image and glory of God, "the effulgence of His glory and the very image (*character*) of His being." (v. 3a.)

From the beginning, the Son participated in the majesty of the divine glory. His royal accession to the right hand of God after He had dealt with our sins (Hebrews 1:3c,d) was a glorifying of the Son with the glory He had with the Father before the world began.

This glory found its effulgence in the Spirit-glory at creation. In creating all things, the Word of God, Who was in the beginning (John 1:1), thus proceeded forth from the Spirit of God — as did also the incarnate Word and the enscripturated Word.

23

We are confronted again with this mystery of the Son's identity with the Spirit, His personal distinctiveness, and His procession from the Spirit in the figure of that angel associated with the glory cloud and called the angel of the presence.

God's theophanic glory is the glory of royal majesty. At the center of the heavens within the veil of the glory cloud is found a *throne*. The glory is "preeminently the place of God's enthronement."[2]

The issue we must deal with in terms of the likeness of the glory is intricately tied to the One Who is seated upon the throne. Ezekiel, in exile by the river Chebar in Babylon and bereft of a temple in which to minister, was inducted instead into the prophetic office by an apprehension of the glory cloud. (Ezekiel 1:1.)

There, he saw the heavens opened (the glory cloud) and had visions of God. The entire first chapter of Ezekiel with all the symbolism and colorful description of wheels, living beings with four faces and wings, chariot movement, crystalline blue pavement, a throne and a MAN, is summed up in the statement: **This was the appearance of the likeness of the glory of the Lord** (Ezekiel 1:28b).

The nature of this vision coincides with the expression and effulgence of the glory of the Son in Hebrews 1. The vision has but one object in view. There is the likeness of a *Man* on the throne of God, the all-governing aspect of the vision.

When viewing the apocalyptic vision of this deported priest, now ordained prophet, in the arid desert of Babylon, there is a clear connection between all the parts of this vision. One cannot separate the living beings from the wheels, from the pavement, from the throne above the pavement, or from the Man on the throne. Everything reveals a unified whole. This is the likeness of the glory of the Lord.

This is the image of God in the Man, and all things are connected to Him. Everything in this vision is moving in synchronous rhythm and harmony. They all originate from the same place, which is due north, and are together moving the same direction to all four points of the compass. A four-fold fullness of revelation of the Man, the glory, and the purpose of the Almighty was opened to Ezekiel, who was referred to repeatedly by the Lord as "son of man."

What governs all true prophetic types regardless of gender, race, class, cultural preference, or denominational preference, is the ability to grasp the vision of the Man on the throne. The government is upon His shoulders. (Isaiah 9:6.) He shared the glory of that throne before the world was. (John 17:5.) He must be seen by all true visionaries in the same place (John 6:62), if they are to speak prophetically to their generations.

As he was being stoned, Stephen attested to this reality when he cried out: **Behold, I see . . . the Son of man standing on the right hand of God** (Acts 7.56.) The essential nature of prophetic ministry is caught up in the One Man on the throne of glory. The Father promised the Son in the eternal councils that His throne would be everlasting: **Thy throne, O God, is for ever and ever** (Psalm 45:6).

The very heart of the Father is tied up in the Son. The Son came forth from the bosom of the Father (John 1:18) and has revealed Him. All things done by God have a paternal overshadowing. The heart of God is the heart of a father. God longs for sons in the image of the One Son.

Since the Spirit of God cries out within all true sons: "Abba, Father" (Romans 8:15), then there indeed must be a seeing and a speaking of that intention in all true prophetic ministry. Anything that falls short of that image will cause those who carry the prophetic vision to cry out and weep for the lack of sight in the people of God.

God's Creation Purpose Is His Image in Man

Spiritual blindness is as possible today as it was in the days of the exile and the deportation of Judah. Few if any were able to see or hear what Jeremiah and Ezekiel saw and

heard. Paul tells us clearly that the mandate and purpose of
the Father is wrapped up in the image of a Man:

> **For whom he did foreknow, he also did
> predestinate to become conformed to the image of his
> Son, that he might be the firstborn** (prototype) **among
> many brethren.**

Romans 8:29

God is after only one thing: "sons" (children) who bear
the image of the glory. It is the business of prophetic ministry to interpret all things in relation to the Man on the throne.
Prophetic insight enables the Church to understand the
implications of former things, latter things, present things,
and all the dynamics in between, to be interpreted from a
unified and spiritual plane.

All things must work together and fit the architectural
framework of the image in the glory cloud if the heart of the
prophet is to be satisfied with what he or she sees in the
visible arena. The prophet lives in close proximity to the Man
on the throne and sees everything in direct relationship to
that invisible reality.

Anything not seen from that plane, whether it be
relational, circumstantial, or situational, has the potential to
fall short of the glory. Anything not seen from that perspective can fail "to work together for good to those who love
Him" (Romans 8:28), as it would not be related and called
according to His purpose.

This matter of spiritual interpretation is essential to the
voice of the prophets. They find no solace in the mundane
or the banal. They are gripped by a vision *alternative to the
reality of the natural world* that counteracts the dominant culture. Brueggemann also wrote:

> The alternative consciousness to be nurtured,
> on the one hand serves to criticize in dismantling
> the dominant consciousness. To that extent, it
> attempts to do what the liberal tendency has done,
> engage in a rejection and delegitimatizing of the

present ordering of things. On the other hand, that alternative consciousness to be nurtured serves to energize persons and communities by its promise of another time and situation toward which the community of faith may move.

To that extent it attempts to do what the conservative tendency has done, live in fervent anticipation of the newness God has promised and will surely give. In thinking this way, the key word is *alternative*, and every prophetic minister and prophetic community must engage in a struggle with that notion.[3]

In the context of Ezekiel's call and dilemma, we see that very thing working its way out into the arena of the disenchanted remnant by the river. This is an exiled people, who lost their *landedness* because they failed to honor and embrace the glory.

As a result, they were delivered over by God to what they really had embraced (whether they consciously realized it or not). The paradigm in which they lived was the dominant culture of the rest of the Middle East where false images and idols were worshipped.

That is why so many of them remained in Babylon seventy years later instead of returning to Judea. They simply took the path of least resistance. It takes great wrenching efforts to accept the earthquake of revelation and change the way one sees the world.

Into that stream of images and oppressive idolatry, God opened the heavens over a young man who was groomed for the priesthood but now had no temple in which to practice his craft. Yet Yahweh, who cannot be limited to structures built for Him by man, is a free agent to move wherever He chooses, as His throne is mobile and the wheels move wherever His Spirit wills.

The momentum of God arrived at the river of exile to enlist a would-be priest, transforming him into a visionary voice to his generation. He was empowered by the Spirit to embody the revelation he saw in vision. He was to call the people to a hope of a return to the enthronement of God in their hearts and, ultimately, to the building of His true temple, where a Man will be seen on the throne.

The liberating power of the vision of glory enabled Ezekiel to be carried by the Spirit into a new dimension of reality, long since abandoned and forgotten because the eyes of the people had lost the ability to *remember* God. They were blind and deaf, having forgotten the God Who formed them (Deuteronomy 32:18) by the manifestation of the glory cloud and the image in the cloud.

[handwritten margin note: who sits enthroned on heart. Heart will be moved by that thing]

The movement of the wheels of His throne toward Ezekiel, who at thirty years of age is primed and ready for service, signified the fresh moving of God on a pliable and virgin generation that would once again see the likeness of the glory and be transformed. The purpose was so all-consuming that the voice of the "new thing" (not new at all to God or to the ancestors), was the alternative consciousness to the dominant culture of exiled confusion.

The disorientation of the circumstances provided the leverage for the reorientation of vision in the mind of first the prophet and then a remnant of the nation. The illusion of the dominant culture served the purpose of God in disillusioning the people, so that as many as would "hear" could be restored to the vision of the Man on the throne. It has ever been, and always will be, the testimony of that Man which God is after.

Image Was Created To Rule Creation

We are told that Elohim said, **Let us make** *man* (Genesis 1:26). There indeed is the image of a man that God is after. This man was formed of dust and had the breath of God infused in him so that he became more alive than he could fathom. (Genesis 2:7.)

This issue of life is wrapped up in the very breath of God, which is the Spirit or wind of God. Man was created to have dominion (rule) over the other living things that God had created. (Genesis 1:26,27.)

> **Thou madest him to have dominion over the works of thy hands; thou hast put all things under his feet:**
>
> **All sheep and oxen, yea, and the beasts of the field;**
>
> **The fowl of the air, and the fish of the sea, and whatsoever passeth through the paths of the seas.**
>
> **Psalm 8:6-8**

All living created things were therefore to be "under his feet" (except other human beings). The man *was* the image, the "shadow" or type of the true image to come, and God's "image" was to have stewardship over the plants and animals of the earth.

This man, this image, is the expression of the mind of God in the context of earthly life. That which we see in "seed" form in Genesis became a metaphor for the spiritual intent of God for us in Christ. The *Man* must be formed in us and revealed in us. This is the **hope of glory** (Colossians 1:27).

Paul gave us insight into his experiential understanding of the dealings and processing of God in his own life and ministry when he wrote:

> **But when it pleased God, who separated me from my mother's womb, and called me by his grace,**
>
> **To reveal his Son *in me*, that I might preach him among the heathen; immediately I conferred not with flesh and blood.**
>
> **Galatians 1:15,16**

This man, this image of God, cannot rule over God's creation in any way except he is ruled himself by God.

As the mind of God is embraced and yielded to, he is able to subdue and have dominion over lesser forms of the creation. If he fails to yield to the mind and image of God, he becomes *as* the lesser creation. He can be likened then to a "horse or mule that needs bit and bridle to be kept in check." (Psalm 32:9.)

All of God's creation is good, but not until the *image* is formed is it **very good** (Genesis 1:31). Even animals intended for the use of man cannot be domesticated for the purpose of service without man. On their own, they wander aimlessly, accomplishing little or nothing of their intended purpose. It is the image-man who is given the mind of God to govern the works of God.

This image in its original form is both male and female. (Genesis 1:27.) Male/female is a full-orbed revelation of the nature and likeness of the Godhead. When the image falls short of the intention, and bows low to worship an image of the creature (Genesis 3:1-7; Romans 1), the intended ruling image becomes marred and is transformed into a falsehood.

Thus man, created to become what is beheld in the glory, became what is beheld in the lower regions, close to the ground, even near to the dust from which his frame was formed. Man then lost the ability to discern the will of Him who formed him.

The Church can fall into a carnal and ambition-driven establishment when it loses its vision of the image of the glory. For this reason, Paul admonished the church at Corinth, addressing them as "mere men," babes in Christ, unspiritual at best, bestial at worst. (1 Corinthians 3:1-3.)

Paul described the nature of spiritual ministry when he wrote:

> **For what man knoweth the things of a man, save the spirit of man which is in him? even so the things of God knoweth no man, but the Spirit of God.**
>
> **Now we have received, not the spirit of the world, but the Spirit which is of God; that we might know the things that are freely given to us of God.**

> **Which things also we speak, not in the words which man's wisdom teacheth, but the Holy Ghost teacheth; comparing spiritual things with spiritual.**
>
> 1 Corinthians 2:11-13

Unfortunately, we have failed to comprehend that this matter of prophetic ministry requires that we be spiritually minded to comprehend the purpose of God. Prophetic ministry is totally governed by the anointing. Prophetic ministry therefore is dependent upon the revelation given by the Spirit of God of the mind of God.

That mind is wrapped up in the image of a MAN. It is for this reason that the *nabiy*, the "seer," could not speak, except he or she *saw* by and in the Spirit. (1 Samuel 9:9; 2 Samuel 15:27; 1 Chronicles 21:9; 2 Chronicles 9:29.) It is the Spirit Who initiates, directs and reveals the mind and nature of God in the earthly vessel that speaks for God.

The Spirit of truth will disclose the testimony of the God-Man, Christ Jesus, to the hungry follower after God. (John 16:13-15.) Until we "see" the image of the Man by the Spirit, we can have nothing whatsoever real or true to say about God, let alone prophesy about. God speaks His Son. (Hebrews 1:1 literally says "God spoke Son.") The language of God is *Son*. All God ever speaks is Son. To not hear that is to have no ears to hear what the Spirit is saying to the Church.

The Apostle John wrote of this principle concerning the testimony of the image very clearly toward the end of his life. When we open the book of Revelation, we discover from the very outset that it involves the "testimony" of (and about) Jesus Christ. (Revelation 1:2.)

Revelation Always "Reveals" Jesus

The entire book, we are told, is a revelation of Jesus, not primarily the revelation of future events. To miss Him is to miss the intent of this monumental prophetic masterpiece. (Revelation 1:1.)

prophetic masterpiece of your life (big picture) artistic & it is all about Jesus. Every stroke of the brush

John made it clear that, because of his stand for Jesus, he had been banished to the island called "Patmos" (a prison island that literally meant "my killing"), appropriately named both naturally and metaphorically. It was perhaps the last outpost of the Roman Empire, sitting in the Aegean Sea west of Asia Minor.

It was used as a penal colony, and Rome's prisoners were consigned to live in caves on the southern part of the island. It was indeed a rugged place, not one that invited a sense of warmth or comfort, but rather invited death itself to take the lives of those exiled there.[4]

John described his ordeal on this isolated place, surrounded by water (chaos), with no means of transport back to a "landed-place," as part of the "journey" through this world that he was called to share with his brethren. He could not have the Kingdom without the tributary distress and patient "hanging in there" that is part and parcel of fellowship in the Gospel. (Revelation 1:9.)

John totally identified with the Church at large in the day-to-day struggles and warfare that accompany this life. John let all future followers of the image know that he was exiled because of "the Word of God and the testimony of Jesus." In other words, his theology put him into exile.

His word about God, connected to this testimony of God's Man, is what got him sent to the place called "My Killing." John voiced no contention with Rome for banishing him. Rather, he saw that he was there because of a revelation of a Man! He worked out his theology in the testimony of this Man. He did not in the least see himself a victim of circumstance but rather as a "shaper" of the future.

He functioned as a prophetic voice. It was this "testimony of Jesus" that filled his heart and mind. John wrote the greatest piece of prophecy in the New Testament-era because he was filled with a staggering vision of a Man. When we read his words towards the end of this moving piece of prophetic poetry we are told:

> And he saith unto me, Write, Blessed are they
> which are called unto the marriage supper of the
> Lamb. And he saith unto me, These are the true
> sayings of God.
>
> And I fell at his feet to worship him. And he
> said unto me, See thou do it not; I am thy
> fellowservant, and of thy brethren that have the
> testimony of Jesus; worship God: for the testimony
> of Jesus is the spirit of prophecy.

Revelation 19:9,10

In other words, the testimony of Jesus is the prophetic spirit. The prophetic anointing is tied to the revelation of the Man on the throne. If we fail to comprehend this, we will reduce this text to a "Pentecostalism"[5] with three levels of prophetic anointing but a poor excuse for exegetical study.

The spirit of prophecy, according to the text, is not when everyone can prophesy because the "anointing is present." This teaching may have helped release some saints to "boldly go where no man has gone before," but it totally ignores the context in which this verse was written.

This statement of John's had nothing to do with a mass or corporate anointing to prophesy. Turn the sentence structure around to truly understand it: **the testimony of Jesus is the spirit of prophecy**. This has to do with the glorious truth that, when the image of God is seen as the Man Christ Jesus revealed in and through the saints, the prophetic spirit is at work.

What the man calling himself "a fellowservant" expressed (v. 10) was so much of the testimony of Jesus that he revealed the Man! That anointing in the fellowservant was so powerful that John wanted to worship him and actually mistook him for Jesus. This I believe is significant.

John knew the Lord intimately while He was on earth. John was the closest to Him of the three of the inner circle (Peter, James, and John). On Patmos, however, in rapturous splendor and the explosion of a fullness of the glory, he did not even recognize the humanity of a fellowservant now glorified and in heaven. He was so mistaken, because the anointing on the man bespoke the nature of Jesus Himself.

The man stopped John from attempting to worship him and explained that what John was experiencing was the very "spirit of prophecy," the testimony of the image in man! Any teaching or belief that reduces this to the occasional exercise of a prophetic utterance in a corporate gathering is a gross reduction, taking away the significance of the text.

When we are enshrouded in the glory, we reveal the Man. It is His testimony in us that glorifies the Father. It is this that the Father is pleased to do, reveal the Son *in* us, and then *through* us. The genuine and mature operation of the prophetic spirit is the testimony of Jesus.

This does not diminish the declaration of the Word of the Lord, for it is the speech of God that releases the glory of God. Rather, we must forsake those "wineskins" that have little ability to be stretched to handle the potency of the new wine. The new wine has the potential of greater glory if allowed to be in a vessel that is stretchable.

Our model, our pattern, must be enlarged if we are to fully comprehend the "spirit of prophecy." It is the very expression, the very testimony of Jesus in the midst of the Church (Revelation 1:12-18), accomplishing His purpose and revealing His presence through a people who have "eyes to see and ears to hear."

The church of every locality addressed in the book of Revelation has a promise to the overcomer. (Revelation 3-5.) The theologian-prophet John voiced the burden of the risen Christ to every church and called for the overcomers to embrace the promise of greater glory. It is consummated in the testimony of Jesus.

In a sermon by T. A. Sparks, delivered more than forty years ago, he discussed the "Persistent Purpose of God":

> The overcomers are those who have put away what is not according to Christ and are now an expression of that Divine Man.[6]

4

The Volume of the Book

> Jesus' primary office is that of *King*. It is to this that his title, "Christ," always points in the New Testament. . . . Jesus is God's vice-regent throughout the universe. (Matthew 28:18; Ephesians 1:22.) As God's Savior-King, Jesus has absolute control over all creatures, and an absolute claim upon men.[1]
>
> — J. L. Packer

The 40th Psalm, a psalm of David, is referred to by the writer of Hebrews. (10:5-7.) The commentary that follows in Hebrews shows us that the psalm is ultimately speaking of Christ and the New Covenant. Once again, we find the testimony of a Man at the very core of revelation.

As a point of consideration and for the purpose of further clarification regarding the testimony of Jesus, which indeed is "the spirit of prophecy," it is essential that we look at the text quoted by the writer to the Hebrews.

Psalm 40:6-8 reads as follows:

> **Sacrifice and offering thou didst not desire; mine ears hast thou opened: burnt offering and sin offering hast thou not required.**
>
> **Then said I, Lo, I come: in the volume of the book it is written of me,**
>
> **I delight to do thy will, O my God: yea, thy law is within my heart.**

This psalm may allude to the restoration of the throne after the short-lived attempt of David's son Absalom to usurp his father's place. Whether David wrote it on this occasion or not, the issue was one of a king giving thanks for deliverance by the hand of the Lord from affliction and then voicing a new dedication and devotion to the service of God.

This "service" had little to do with the regimented rituals of the Law, namely sacrifices and offerings on the altar. Rather, it referred to doing the will of the Father by "opening" the spiritual ear of the king to His Word and the very Law being found in his heart. David aspired to the "testimony of Jesus." It is the Ideal Man that he was longing to become.

In and of himself this was utterly impossible, but for the believer in Christ, this is our inheritance. The total obedience of Jesus made the need for external sacrifice totally obsolete. David longed for something as man that only one Man could achieve. However, that One Man's future work, His achievement, would be accounted to (credited to) all who believe on Him.

The purpose of Christ coming into the world was to recover *that which* (not "those who") was lost. (Luke 19:10.) This matter of recovery is tied indeed to the testimony of God in the earth, which is always manifest as a demonstration of the Spirit and of power. (1 Corinthians 2:1-4.)

The "volume of the book" relates to the coming of the One Who would be a living demonstration of the testimony of God *in* a Man *for* man. When the psalmist declared, **Lo, I come; in the volume of the book it is written of me**, the context was in response to the "piercing of his ear," as when a servant voluntarily became a bondslave. (Exodus 21:6.) Paul called himself a "bondslave" to Christ.

A Hebrew slave could choose out of love for his master not to be free(d) in the seventh (Jubilee) year, and thus become a lifelong servant of his master. The following custom was observed in such a case: **Then thou shalt take an aul,**

and thrust it through his ear unto the door, and he shall be thy servant for ever (Deuteronomy 15:17).[2]

The "roll of the book," referring to the parchment roll containing the portion of Scripture the psalmist was prepared to obey, may in fact be a reference to Deuteronomy 17:14-20. Those verses delineated the responsibility of the king to the land and the people, and in fact, his relationship to the prophet as well.

The king's duties were clearly expressed in terms of the stewardship of inheritance based on the revelation of the Torah. In fact, the kings of Israel were supposed to serve as "types," shadows, or pictures of the one true King to come.

The challenge to Samuel for a king arose in the acquisition of land for Israel and the temptation to want a king "like the other nations" once they were landed. (1 Samuel 8:5,20.) For Israel, being "landed" was their supreme anticipation. Their sojourn from Abraham to Moses had been spent in anticipation of land, and finally, Joshua brought a generation born in the wilderness into the covenantal promise.

However, once in the land and after the Israelites had died who remembered the taking of the land and those who took it, succeeding generations forgot Yahweh and suffered repeated judgment for their sins. When they were at last exiled from the land, they again longed for a sense of being "landed." To this day, land issues are the seed-bed of turmoil in the Middle East.

Forgetting the Past Is a Great Mistake

For us in Christ, the "land" is a type of our spiritual inheritance in the heavenly realms. Our "heavenly Joshua" (*Jesus* is the Greek transliteration of *Joshua*) has, by His complete obedience, brought us into our inheritance. We are heirs of the Father and joint-heirs with the Son. (Romans 8:17) As a result, we have insight into the mystery of God, which is Christ, the Man/King, in us, the desired expectation of glory. (Colossians 1:27.)

As we consider the "shadow" (under the old economy), we can gain insight into the "substance" (under the new economy), which belongs to Jesus.

The people of God who entered the promised land under the Mosaic economy needed to make proper choices for the future based on their knowledge of God's dealings with them in the past. Under the new economy, we entered through our heavenly Joshua a land of "promises," so that by them we might become partakers of the divine nature (2 Peter 1:3-9) — but we are not to forget from whence we came.

Israel forgot God and forfeited their inheritance. They mismanaged the land they were given. There is abundant testimony in Scripture of the failure of their kings to rule after the heart of God, which Samuel had prophesied would be the case. (1 Samuel 8:11-18.)

In fact, most of the time there was a tension between the kings and the true prophets of God. Whereas the priesthood should have experienced the counsel of peace between the two offices of king and priest (Zechariah 6:13), there was instead turmoil and violation resulting in enmity between true prophets and unyielding kings.

Wandering in the wilderness had a set of rules to govern a wilderness paradigm. Inheritance of land brought with it a new paradigm, and as a result a new set of rules under which to function.

The rules that governed life in the wilderness were different from the rules that governed life in the land. In the wilderness all things were managed by the nurturing hand of God in the glory cloud. All provision was tied up in the cloud, as the wilderness was a howling waste and void of enough plant, animal, and bird life to sustain the nation. (Deuteronomy 32:10.)

Once landed, however, the manna ceased falling from the cloud, and the land yielded produce in abundance. (Joshua 5:12.) The Israelites had to then learn to discern the movements of God in less spectacular but no less super-natural ways, as they co-labored with Him in the fellowship of His ultimate intention.

The throne was not meant to be an "untouchable" place, where the king would demand obedience as a king did in other nations and rule by oppression. Rather, the throne was to be a place for "one of the brethren" (Deuteronomy 17:14), not a foreigner. This "one" was to have his memory filled with past experiences of the community as a whole and his heart "circumcised" by the flint of affliction.

The king was supposed to understand, first of all, the way God brought the nation from aloneness and faith as a sojourner with Abram to the brickyard of Pharaoh, where the exploitation of blessing was the means of increasing another's coffers. The elect were in bondage because a Pharaoh came to power who feared them, when he saw they were blessed and becoming powerful. (Exodus 1:7-10.)

One who would rule as king over Israel or Judah ought to have this in his memory, lest he forget that he too could easily exploit those who lived in his kingdom. The seat of authority was *not* to mold the character of the man:

The character of the man was to mold the seat of authority.

Whoever took the throne by appointment in the nation was to do so in the context of covenant. "One of us" was to be on the throne. One who had processed the pain of the past with them. One who had learned to rule his spirit and trust in Yahweh, therefore to do justice, love loyalty, and walk humbly before God. (Micah 6:8.)

The issue for the one enthroned was not control or power, but management and enhancement of the inherit-ance for the benefit of those whom he was to serve.[3]

Most Kings Ruled by Fear and Control

In Deuteronomy 17, kings also were forbidden to multiply wives, gold, or horses. Amassing all of those was a common practice in ancient times and in some areas of the world today. A ruler adding to his possessions operated in a model of fear and control, the common lot of nations whose God was not the Lord. The outward reasons for these actions by kings were:

• The multiplication of wives had to do with the marrying of daughters of foreign kings to ensure peace between the nations.

• The multiplication of gold had to do with the building of one's own kingdom at the expense of those who labored for the king.

• The multiplication of horses was for the express purpose of increasing military power in the event of an attack from opposing armies.

In Israel, however, a king was not to intermarry with foreign wives regardless of the political benefits, because to do so would bring a defiling and idolatrous spirit into the nation. However, as we can see from reading the history of Israel and Judah, their kings in general did not heed the word of the Lord.

The gods of surrounding nations became part of the culture of Israel. The "baals" (lords of various aspects of nature) worked their way into Israelite history through kings marrying the daughters of foreigners who worshipped them, setting examples for the people to do likewise.

So, too, the temptation to rely on military superiority to guarantee safety in the nation overrode faith in an invisible God named Yahweh. Soldiers, chariots, and horses gave the people a visible means of defense. This occurred in spite of Yahweh's declaring in many ways: . . . **Not by might, nor by power** (armies), **but by my spirit, saith the Lord of hosts** (Zechariah 4:6), or "heavenly armies."

The intention and promise of the covenant-making and keeping God was to be their true King and protector. His angelic guardians were more than sufficient to keep Israel. David said of Him, **He that keepeth Israel shall neither slumber nor sleep** (Psalm 121:4).

"Gold and silver" really involved an issue of trust in terms of who would provide for the future of the "dynasty." Whose dynasty was it anyway? If it was the king's own, then he had best fill his pockets for the long haul, but if the dynasty was God's, then His provision was to be faithful to the thousandth generation. (Deuteronomy 7:9.) The same is true for us today.

The essential responsibility of the one enthroned was to lay hold of the scriptures in the presence of the priests and make a copy of a portion of it in a book for himself. In "the volume" of that book, he was to meditate on a daily basis:

• He was to reflect on the collective memory and history of the people whom he ruled, all the while remembering that he also was one of them.

• He was to govern his life, as well as the kingdom, according to the mandates of the Torah (the Jewish term for the Old Testament, not all of which had been written then).

• He was to assimilate into his decision-making process the memories of the sojourn of faith from barrenness to birth, from famine to provision, and from slavery to freedom.

• He was to be reminded always of the admonition of Moses at the edge of the wilderness overlooking the promised land.

• He was to remember the Lord God, remember his brethren, and do all that was in "the volume of the book." In this way, he would ensure the prosperity of the next generation and generations to come.

The throne was governed by a revelation from God. The "volume of the book" was simply to supply the essential vision for rule and power. The book revealed how kings were to reign righteously and steward the land for the next generation. The great tragedy of Israel, and later, Judah, is that the majority of their kings never were governed by the divine intention.

Even the great and wise Solomon committed all three sins that kings ought not commit. He multiplied wives to himself, and following the visit of the Queen of Sheba, he multiplied gold to himself (666 shekels), and horses, in direct violation of God's mandate in Deuteronomy 17:14-17. (2 Chronicles 9:13-28.)

Solomon Became a Negative Model

Solomon became, in a very real sense, a type of anti-christ. He is the epitome of what kings were not to be. While there are some very profound truths that can strengthen our understanding of the potential of Kingdom dynamics in the picture of the Temple of Solomon, we must realize that he became corrupted by his pursuit of all that was in the world.

Ecclesiastes is the commentary of a man who filled his life with everything he could desire and came close to losing his own soul. He forsook "the volume of the book," and within two years of his death, his son lost the ability to hold the kingdom together. The kingdom of Israel split into two nations as a result of the pride and arrogance of Solomon and Rehoboam, who listened to greedy court followers and not to the priests and wise men. (2 Chronicles 10:1-19.)

The sins of Solomon were the root cause of the later years of spiritual decline, which brought captivity and enslavement once again. A people once landed were ultimately deported to Assyria (the ten-tribed nation of Israel) and lost from view, and to Babylon (basically Judah and Benjamin), from where "a remnant" returned. The sins of these "fathers" affected all future generations of Israelites.

From a perspective regarding the prophetic framework of things it becomes evident that "not all that glitters is gold." A king who failed to be governed by "the volume of the book" lost the prophetic authority to take a people into the future. The journey into the future was to be built on the memory of the past. The collective memory of the nation as told by the Torah was the assurance of consistency and substance for the future.

All that is to be anticipated in the future for anyone or any nation is connected to what is remembered from the past. For a king to reign, he must see the river as it flows from the source in order to understand the course it takes to where it empties into the sea.

For the fullness of the spirit of prophecy, the testimony of a Man, there must come a harmonizing of the offices of king, priest, and prophet. The perpetuation of the throne from past to future is rooted in Torah. The root word in the Hebrew for Torah is *yarah*. It implies the throwing of a javelin that will hit the intended mark.

In essence, the word of Yahweh is for each who will hear it a dart thrown by an expert marksman, namely God Himself, designed to direct one's life so that it will hit its intended goal. If we fail to follow the path of the dart, we "miss the mark," as sin is referred to in the New Covenant. (Romans 3:23.)

The trajectory of a javelin, dart, or even an arrow is first determined by a pulling back prior to a thrusting forward. The marksman draws the dart back behind him, then releases it with a span of force that encloses the marksman behind and before. The length, speed, and accuracy of the throw of the dart or the release of the arrow is tied to the backward pull that initiates the forward momentum.

The anticipated future, the intended end, the plans for a radically new tomorrow in God are tied to the backward pull of the history of a people and the backward pull of eternity past. A king would fail to anticipate a future with prophetic insight, if he failed to take with him the "backward pull" of the Torah, the *yarah*, of Israel's history in God.

A king was to hold prophetic glory in creative tension. That creative tension exists between a remembered past and an anticipated future. To "miss the mark" is to forget the former and thus forfeit the latter. The NOW of God (Hebrews 11:1) is a substantive moment in the present that contains the fullness of God's intention, because it stretches from the beginning to the end and encompasses everything in between.

There can be no shaping of destiny without a recollecting of history. For the king to fail to realize that the NOW of faith was pregnant with a glorious future because it was conceived in a historic past, was to minimalize the present. He ended up reigning by control rather than management. To forget the Torah was to delegitimize the eternity of God, whose endings are always in His beginnings.

The king who sat on the throne was merely a symbol of the King who sits enthroned in glory. His throne was established from "of old" according to the Psalms. (Psalm 93:2.) All time is NOW with the Almighty, therefore the eternity of God governs those things which take place in the time-space continuum. The completed plan and the complete Man are ever before Him.

God's endings are always in His beginnings. To be true to the divine trust, then, a king must be governed by the Torah, for in its beginnings were the ultimate endings of God. In its past was the people's future.

Forgetting the Word Meant Forfeiting the Land

To forget the Torah was to wrongly perceive the purpose of either the throne or the inheritance. Kings and prophets should have worked side by side building for the future because they were energized by the past. Instead, there was great tension between the two offices throughout the flow of biblical history.

By the season of Christ's first coming, the king already had sold out to other nations, the priesthood had learned to control rather than lead, and the Prophet must live in the wilderness until the day of His public appearing.

In the day of Messiah's appearing, the Word was not in the mouth of the king, for he had attempted to murder the true Seed of royalty in order to perpetuate his own kingdom. (Matthew 2:16-18.) Herod the Great may have had a

Jewish mother (an Idumean father), but apparently he had little or no knowledge of the Torah.

In fact, he had priests study the scriptures for him to verify the validity of Messianic hope and the prophesied whereabouts of His beginnings. (Matthew 2:3,4.) If he had truly been governed by the Torah, there was no reason to make inquiry elsewhere, for the future already was written in the past.

Kings and priests were already ideologically too far apart for a reconciliation. Only in the final hours of Jesus' passion at the very seat of Pilate, did the "kings" and the priests find something to work together to accomplish: the death of the Son of Man.

The priesthood had no substance whatsoever in terms of the ability to discern the spiritual season in which they lived. In actual fact, at a time when the word of the Lord should have been with them and in them, it was withdrawn from their mouths and placed in the mouth of a prophet who remained "outside the royal court." (Luke 3:1,2.)

John the Baptist, the voice of recovery, moving in the spirit and power of Elijah (Matthew 11:14; Malachi 4:5), stood totally outside the place of the "status quo." He not only stood outside the royal court, but appeared on the "other side" of the Jordan, outside the land, for the king and the priests had negated the right to the land and the temple. Within the span of that generation they would lose both once again. (Matthew 24:15-21.)

That which corrupt kings and priests preferred to disregard, prophets continued to honor. They were consumed with "the volume of the book." The heart of the prophet was for the recovery of the Lord's testimony in all its completeness and intention. The loss of vision, the loss of intention, is all tied to the misapprehension of what was recorded in "the volume of the book."

Jesus Himself prophesied over Jerusalem and its inhabitants shortly before the crucifixion:

> O Jerusalem, Jerusalem, thou that killest the
> prophets, and stonest them which are sent unto thee,
> how often would I have gathered thy children
> together, even as a hen gathereth her chickens under
> her wings, and ye would not!
>
> Behold, your house is left unto you desolate.
>
> Matthew 23:37,38

The One Who came and governed His life by what was
written in "the volume of the book," born as a King-Priest
after an uncommon order, raised up also as Prophet, declared
that after His departure, all Jerusalem would have left would
be the form of godliness. Prophetic presence would depart,
leaving the house (temple and city) absolutely desolate.

Jesus Is the End and the Beginning

The synergizing of the three offices in the One Man,
God's Son, indicates that the fullness of "the volume of the
book" spoke of the all-encompassing, the utterly comprehensive, nature of Jesus. The prophet was particularly for
the land and the land was for the prophet. In Deuteronomy
18:9 and 15, we read:

> When thou art come into the land which the Lord
> thy God giveth thee, thou shalt not learn to do after
> the abominations of those nations. . .

> The Lord thy God will *raise up* unto thee a
> Prophet from the midst of thee, of thy brethren, like
> unto me; unto him ye shall hearken.

It is worth noting that the prophet was not chosen
by the people (as some of the kings were) but rather was
raised up by God. Peter quoted this text and gave direct
reference to the *resurrection of Christ*. (Acts 3:22,26.) Moses
prophesied both of Jesus being nurtured in the land during
His hidden years and being raised up to be the voice of God,
as well as having been "buried" in the land as a Seed.

He was raised incorruptible and declared with power
to be the Son of God, Who thus has authority to give life or

destroy life. Prophets are intended to address kings. This One addressed more than earthly potentates, He addressed principalities and powers and overthrew all the powers of hell itself in His rising from the dead. (Colossians 2:15.)

Consider these words of Walter Brueggemann regarding the prophet, according to the Deuteronomical text (Deuteronomy 18:9-22):

> The land and the illusion of self-sufficiency seduced and lulled people into managing their lives and their land in ways that seem beyond the terrors of history. The prophet, by contrast, is Israel's single source of insight and guidance. He existed to affirm continually to Israel its precariousness and contingency in the face of more attractive but illegitimate alternatives. The prophet was intended precisely for speech (a) in the land, (b) in the face of the king, (c) against idolatrous forms of self-securing. . . .

> The prophet neither stood rooted in the model of "other nations" nor selected by Israel like a king. He was, by contrast, *raised up by Yahweh*. The language of resurrection is used to announce this one who strangely and peculiarly derives authority from Yahweh as does none other. But he has one important point of commonality with the king. He also is "from among you, from your brethren," that is, he is steeped in covenant and prepared to speak out of it. . . .

> He can come only out of the life and faith and history of Israel with Yahweh. He is designed to articulate that consciousness against all other seductions of power and security. He is to assure that the land be discerned in covenantal ways. Thus the meeting of king and prophet provides a paradigm for one with "lifted heart" and one "raised by Yahweh," one a self-securing manager, the other committed to land as a gift.[4]

The shape and structure of church life and history are rooted in our "landedness." In other words, the place we have been given as a gift by God, in Christ, is to be valued as such, stressing the relationship between brethren and inheritance.

The soil, the seed, and the workers were, and are, all to be networked in an over-arching framework that pulls all things together in the context of covenant. Kings, priests, and prophets were to work side by side, in relation to what was written in the "volume of the book," and thus manage and steward the inheritance for the sake of the future.

God has shut up all facets of the governance of His people until the second "fulness of times" (Ephesians 1:10), when His Son, the express image of His glory comes again as Prophet, Priest, and King to give His people their inheritance and manage it for them, with them, and through them, in order for the vision of God to be realized (fulfilled) in them.

5
The Matter of Interpretation

> . . . Twentieth-century Christians are used to
> discussing worldview questions in the language
> of philosophy, while the Bible sets forth its
> worldview very often in the language of visual
> imagery (symbolism) and repeated patterns
> (typology) . . . .[1]
>
> — James Jordan

The context from which the prophet of old spoke was
the context of his life and the processing of God to see all
things from a heavenly perspective. In the New Covenant,
while the function is categorically different in terms of the
declaration of the Word of God — in that the Old Testament
prophets for the most part were chosen to pen the Scriptures — there indeed are similarities.

The prophetic voice is involved in the interpretation of
all things from a spiritual perspective in the midst of the
circumstances of life itself. Abraham J. Heschel has written:

> The prophet is a person, not a microphone.
> He is endowed with a mission, with the power of
> a word not his own that accounts for his great-
> ness. However, he or she also has temperament,
> concern, character, and individuality. As there was
> no resisting the impact of divine inspiration, so at
> times there was no resisting the vortex of his own
> temperament. The Word of God reverberates in the
> voice of a man. . . .

The prophet's task is to convey a *divine view,* yet as a person he *is* a point of view. He speaks from the perspective of God as perceived from the perspective of his own situation.[2]

The prophet also sees things that others fail to observe. Prophetic insight enables the Church to understand the implications of past, present, and future issues, events, relationships, and dynamics from a heavenly plane. There is a very real interpretation of the mind of God to the people of God. Those apprehended for such a task are of necessity built and processed to empower them to interpret things in such a fashion.

The tendency for us in the times in which we live is to continue to "systematize" our theologies so that our presuppositions fit the framework of the Scripture as we see it. However, the architectural framework for prophetic insight requires a restructuring of the imagination to fit a biblical worldview instead of restructuring the Word to fit our beliefs and opinions.

Our systems can help us form doctrinal preferences and assist us in drawing theological "lines in the sand," but they cannot account for the fact that a large portion of the Scripture is woven out of symbol and metaphor. The matter of interpretation requires an understanding of figurative language.

When we attempt to force texts to fit our systematic hermeneutic, we violate the beauty of many portions of Holy Writ. The Master Himself, along with the Apostle Paul, would fail some courses in modern seminaries — both liberal and evangelical — because of our mistaken interpretations of certain texts.

Language rich in metaphor and symbol defies the controlling efforts of man to force the picture to fit a doctrinal position. The tendency and presence of *reductionism* is the very downfall of the modern church and contributes to its spiritual anemia.

In the promise of the outpouring of the Spirit, the very nature of the Spirit's coming was tied to the enlarging of the imaginational faculties of the people. They were to see visions and dream dreams, and to prophesy. (Joel 2:28,29.)

In actual fact the "servants and handmaids" were not to speak prosaically, but rather, poetically. They were, by words rich in image and metaphor, to shape the thoughts of a people and influence their future by the empowering presence of God.

The writings of Thomas Aquinas, the 12th century father of modern rationalism, have done much to influence and even suppress the essential nature of imaginal reality in much modern theology. Scripture, however, is not to be approached as though one were reading the *New York Times*, or other such carefully planned prose.

Such language is far too restrictive for the all-encompassing, multi-faceted Word of the living God. The prophet has had his or her worldview shattered, restructured, and reshaped by the intrusive presence of the Spirit. The unseen has become as real and perhaps more real than the seen.

Consider also that a logically minded, rational approach to Scripture will seek to scientifically relate to the natural world and look at any related material from a biological perspective. However, physicist Donald M. MacKay says:

> "Man's chief end is to glorify God and to enjoy Him forever" . . . [This is] the rubric under which the Christian must practice his science.[3]

While the Creator is the originator and source of all true science, He speaks to us of the animal kingdom, for example, not in terms of how He structured them biologically, but of how they symbolize concepts of "clean" or "unclean."

He uses animals in their symbolic significance in terms of proximity to the tabernacle and the glory in the midst of the people. We are enjoined to observe their "ways" and learn from their patterns of behavior. (Proverbs 30:24-31.)

Restoration Rests on Spiritual Understanding

Consider for a moment the issue of interpretation from a spiritual plane in the context of the story in Mark 8:22-26:

> And he cometh to Bethsaida ("house of snares")[4]; and they bring a blind man unto him, and besought him to touch him.
>
> And he took the blind man by the hand, and led him out of the town; and when he had spit on his eyes, and put his hands upon him, he asked him if he saw ought.
>
> And he looked up, and said, I see men *as trees*, walking.
>
> After that he put his hands again upon his eyes, and made him look up: and he was restored, and saw every man clearly.
>
> And he sent him away to his house, saying, Neither go into the town, nor tell it to any in the town.

A cursory overview of the text would undoubtedly bring one not accustomed to the language of symbol and metaphor to an erroneous conclusion about the nature and meaning of this "sign" from Jesus.

In order to do justice to the text, we must not look at what happened as if Jesus *had* to touch the man more than once because His first touch did not accomplish the task. Instead, we must realize Who Jesus really is and see clearly everything He did in the process of healing the man.

From a prophetic perspective the entire passage is about the changing of a paradigm, a worldview, and the healing and restructuring of imaginal thought. The "house of snares" is the place where the man's problems began. At the end of the story, he is instructed not to go back to the village; in essence, not to fall back into the very paradigm that caused his blindness.

Secondly, we know from the text by implication that to associate trees with men walking implies that he knew what both men and trees looked like. That indicates that he once was able to see and had some framework from which to interpret reality.

However, the fact that he sees them as *trees walking* prior to seeing them clearly after a second and totally restoring touch from Jesus, indicates that the symbolic significance of trees has a great deal to do with how God restructures our imaginations. Until we comprehend the spiritual dimension of men as trees, we will not see them clearly.

Restoration is not possible in terms of a clear vision of God's intention for humanity until we see "men as trees." From the earliest portions of Scripture, trees play a predominant role. They filled the Garden of Delight east of Eden and were for man's physical benefit, as well as to satisfy his field of vision aesthetically. (Genesis 2:9.)

There were two trees in particular given attention in the account of creation that are highly symbolic and necessary to the proving of obedience in Adam: the tree of life and the tree of the knowledge of good and evil. These two trees provided an arena for the outworking of a series of choices whereby Adam was to turn innocence into holiness.

Tragically, Adam failed the probationary test, was expelled from the Garden of Delight, and the ground which once brought forth beautiful things was subjected to futility. It henceforth brought forth thorns and thistles and had to be plowed "by the sweat of Adam's brow." (Genesis 3:17-19.)

The recovering and restoring work of God, however, will transplant man as a tree by irrigation canals in the midst of dry ground so that he can bring forth fruit once again from the sanctuary of God. (Psalm 1.)[5] Ultimately, God brought forth a Tree that healed man.

The root of David, the stem of Jesse, came up out of parched and dry ground, already having been cursed. The Tree of Life Himself became as we are to reverse the curse and heal us in order to restore us back to the Father's original intention. (Isaiah 11:1,2, 53:2.)

If we fail to see the underlying significance of the man seeing men as "trees walking," the *sign* has failed to point us in the direction of clear vision. Prophetic ministry is indeed a matter of the interpretation of all things from a spiritual perspective.

To "see" in the Spirit, requires understanding the invisible attributes of God by the visible things that are made. (Romans 1:20.) It requires not suppressing what we "see" in nature but honoring God because of it and giving thanks in order that the spiritual, invisible world from which the created world came can be grasped and entered into. (Hebrews 11:3.)

> For instance, modern man takes part of the truth about the arrangement of the universe — that is peppered with various kinds of suns called stars, arranged into galaxies, and so forth — and uses the truth to suppress the more important truth that the heavens declare God's glory, and that the heavenly bodies were made for signs and seasons.[6]

Interpretation Controls Understanding

Our failure to "hear" the voice of the prophets with all our spiritual senses is to suffer the loss of their intended message (Acts 13:27), even while their words still ring in our ears. This matter of interpretation is tied to the issue of recovery.

The story in Mark's gospel of the blind man is intended to give us a new worldview. Hopefully, the "house of snares" that blinded men from seeing the glory of God in the face of Christ (2 Corinthians 4:4) will no longer have a hold on our imaginal reality.

Imagination in its true function is not the wishful seeing of something that does not exist, but rather the intuitive awareness of the unseen, yet real, arena of the Spirit. The restructuring of the imagination, the healing of the split between mind and heart, the integrating of the personality to a level of wholeness, is essential to the recovery of the image of God in man.

For that reason, the prophetic ministry must first be processed through the dealings of God in order to see the unseen. *Matters of interpretation are matters of perspective.*

Even Isaiah, in full vision of the Man on the throne, is made acutely aware of his own spiritual sensory deprivation. His conclusion is his utter uncleanness and lack of insight. The end result of the vision is the awareness of the need for a "seeing eye," a "hearing ear," and an "awakened heart." (Isaiah 6:1-7.)

To fail to apprehend the vision is to fail to make the necessary adjustment in worldview. Without such an adjustment, all interpretation is invalid as far as God is concerned. Having eyes we see not, having ears we hear not, lest we see with our eyes, hear with our ears, understand with our hearts, repent (be totally turned around, making a major paradigm shift) and become whole.

Indeed, the whole issue regarding prophetic ministry is a matter of spiritual interpretation, through processed vessels who themselves entered into the journey towards wholeness.

> Now we have received, not the spirit of the world, but the spirit which is of God; that we might know the things that are freely given to us of God.
>
> Which things also we *speak*, not in the words which man's wisdom teacheth, but which the Holy Ghost teacheth; comparing *spiritual things with spiritual* (A more accurate translation of the italicized words is "interpreting spiritual things to spiritual men").
>
> **1 Corinthians 2:12,13**

6

The Council of Jehovah

Prophets had to be people of outstanding character, great minds, and courageous souls. . . . being dedicated to God, they became still greater because of the tasks and special provisions assigned them. Thus they became the towering giants of Israel, the formers of public opinion, the leaders through days of darkness, people distinguished from all those about them either in Israel or other nations of the day.[1]

— Dr. Leon J. Wood

The most significant event for the prophet of old was that moment when, by divine appointment, he was caught up into the Shekinah. For the prophet to be caught up into the cloud was to be actually welcomed into the throne room and to participate with the heavenly Council.

The prophet Jeremiah uttered these words:

> For who has stood in the council of the Lord so as to see and to hear his word? Who has given heed to his word so as to proclaim it?

Jeremiah 23:18 NRSV

The thing which distinguished a true prophet from a false prophet was that the true prophet had actually been "taken up" into the immediate presence of the glory and beheld God in the midst of the angelic guardians and the Council of heaven. False prophets had not had such an

57

experience and, therefore, could not legitimately speak on behalf of heavenly things.

While some of the prophets of old (Isaiah, Ezekiel) have left detailed descriptions of their encounters with God in the glory cloud, others only referred to such an encounter (as with the above example of Jeremiah).

When Isaiah served as prophet to Uzziah, there came a time when this godly king who had brought many reforms to the nation overstepped his sphere of responsibility. There ensued a period of grief in the land and in the prophet's life. In violation of divine ordinance, Uzziah, king of Judah, assumed an anointing he did not possess. As a result of attempting to fill the role of a priest, he was stricken with leprosy and died still a leper some time later. (2 Chronicles 26:16-21.)

There is a tendency to believe that thrones are impervious to mortality and failure. People assume there is safety in official rule and bureaucracy. There are resources available to kings that are not available to the rest of the community. It is the very nature of national authorities to at times presume that, because of "the robes and the throne," there are no boundaries to their exercise of authority.

Yet all earthly thrones are only to serve as representatives of the heavenly throne and of the One occupying it. (Romans 13:1.) When kings failed under the old economy, there were always prophets to either correct or declare the need for repentance, or perhaps issue verdicts of death.

The failure of the kings is evident even by scant observation of the books of Kings and Chronicles. Few if any of the kings truly followed God in comparison to the many who aborted or perverted their mandate, found in Deuteronomy 17:14-20.

The tragedy was that Uzziah had for the most part brought many great reforms to the nation and had been responsible for a restoration of divine order. In a sense, there was a season of reviving under the rule of Uzziah. He also amassed territory that had been lost, so that with the territory of the northern kingdom of Israel, the Israelites ruled as much land as they had under the United Monarchy of David and Solomon.[2]

When, however, he "became strong" (proudful in his deeds), his heart was "lifted up" causing him to ignore the clear instructions of God. (Jeremiah 23:16.) He was struck in judgment and lost his future.

For Isaiah, the fall and death of this king meant the possible loss of kingdom territory and all the reforms for which he had labored so dearly in cooperation with Uzziah. However, Uzziah's son Jotham, who took the throne as soon as his father retired with leprosy, seemed to be following in his father's ways. (2 Chronicles 26:21, 27:1-6).

Another reason for Isaiah's deep grief may have been that he was a close companion of Uzziah, as Isaiah was "a stately gentleman" equally at home in the royal court and the temple environs. He was of a socially prominent family.[3] For almost a year after Uzziah's death, or well into a year, Uzziah's sin of presumption and consequent judgment had a devastating effect on the prophet, then a young man beginning his long career.

We must also assume that the nation as a whole was mourning. Uzziah was only the second leader in the history of the Israelites to be stricken with leprosy for presumption. The first had been Moses' sister Miriam, who was forgiven and restored. (Numbers 12:10-15.)

Uzziah was the tenth king of Judah, after Israel had been divided into two kingdoms, and only the second of those kings to be struck by the Lord in judgment. (2 Chronicles 21:14,15,18,19.) The Judaites lived in a mixture of idolatry and true worship, but had not yet become totally hardened to Yahweh's word. Many of them must have grieved over the Uzziah's sin of presumption and what it might mean to the nation.

It was during this season of grief that Isaiah had a life-transforming experience. At an unexpected moment he was translated into another realm and found himself "caught up" to another throne room, in which he beheld the glory of the Lord, and saw the Lord in session with the heavenly Council.

This marked the qualifying and the commissioning of the prophet. He was sent by the Council to accomplish the purpose of God for both his generation and following generations.

(Once again I would refer the reader to Meredith Kline[4] for a consideration of the "Us" in both Genesis 1:26 and Isaiah 6:8 as showing that the heavenly Court consisted not merely of the Triune God, but also of the attendants around the throne.)

Prophetic Ministry Emerges in Times of Crisis

Prophetic ministry more often than not arose in the midst of "endings" which occurred in the nations of Israel and Judah. Ezekiel had been among the exiles and, like Isaiah, was enduring an even greater time of loss and grief when he was "caught up" into the glory cloud. Ezekiel was living out the prophecies of Isaiah and Jeremiah, which foretold the horrible destruction of Judah and the exile of the survivors of both Israel and Judah.

There in the presence of the Shekinah, Ezekiel perceived the movings and goings of God and saw the "likeness of a Man" on the throne. He observed the absolute harmony with which the living beings, the wheels, and all the attendants moved with the will of the One enthroned above the cherubim. (Ezekiel 1:1-28.)

Even Moses could not lead the people to their destiny apart from being "caught up" into the pillar of cloud and fire. He had to receive a revelation of the mystery of God and instruction while in the presence of the heavenly Council for a "pattern" to be built on earth. (Exodus 24:18.)

The call of Moses was a result of the blood covenant between God and Abraham with its promises and was precipitated by the grief and pain of the Israelites in a crisis situation in Egypt. God's fulfillment of His promise to Abraham concerning the land (Genesis 13:14-17) led to an ending of Egyptian bondage and the beginning of the reign of God in their midst as a nation. (Exodus 3:7-9.)

When Moses was taken into the cloud en route to Canaan, it marked the transitional point at which a pattern (the Tabernacle) emerged that was to testify on the earth as to what governs things in heaven. It also marked the transition of the Israelites from a tribal people to a nation under God.

Centuries later, in the northern kingdom of Israel, the prophet Elijah declared to King Ahab that, just as the king had high court officials around his throne to offer advice, the prophet stood in the presence of Jehovah. Elijah implied that he was a participant in the Council, and on behalf of the Council was making known the decree of the throne. He also implied that the authority of the throne backed up his word. (1 Kings 17:1.)

The emergence of Elijah on the scene occurred during a season of famine and grief in the hearts of the people due to their having forsaken the Lord. Elijah's ministry was formed out of the "pathos of God," as Abraham Heschel would call it, and the grief of 7,000 godly dwellers in Israel who had not bowed the knee to serve the baals. (1 Kings 19:18.)

Administrators and judges served as messengers of the kings' council in the old economy. This structure is still operative today in nations that have functional monarchies. There are some nations where the monarchy is a figurehead and has little real governing power. However, in a nation where a king or queen is indeed ruling, one would find the council on hand to help in the arbitration of matters and the carrying out of decrees.

For Jehovah, the prophet was more than merely a messenger. The prophet stood in the divine Council and was a participant in the activity that took place there. The prophet had sanctuary privilege. While the thought may seem radical to our Western concept of the issue of sovereignty, we must carefully examine the nature of God's choosing to have personal "confidantes" under the old economy. It is also imperative that we discover the New Testament fulfillment of that concept in terms of the Church.

Consider this thought in its Biblical context:

> **And the scripture was fulfilled which saith, Abraham believed God, and it was imputed** (accounted) **unto him for righteousness: and he was called the Friend of God.**
>
> **James 2:23**

Someone in the ancient world called "friend of the king" was a high court official, probably the king's confidential advisor.[5] Moses was called God's friend: **Thus the Lord used to speak to Moses face to face, as one speaks to a friend** (Exodus 33:11 NRSV). Moses was a close companion or confidante of God, and the prophets were raised up by God in the pattern of Moses.

Amos told us clearly, relating to the divine Council, that God will not do anything without revealing it to the prophets, His friends! (Amos 3:7.) As God's confidantes, prophets acted as magistrates, arbiters, referees in certain situations, and at times, even prevailed with God for the people.[6]

Perhaps one of the most revealing scenes in regards to the heavenly Council and participation in it is found in Zechariah. (Zechariah 3:6,7.) The context again is a time of spiritual declension. The remnant of the Jews had returned from Babylonian exile after 70 years, and there was a need for the recovery of the spiritual nature of things in the community of God.

The young prophet was given a series of visions in order to help him further the purpose of God in his time. In standing alongside the aged Prophet Haggai, he was commissioned to motivate the people to recover that which had been lost in their desire to rebuild the house of the Lord.

Joshua, the high priest of the time (a type and picture of Jesus), was seen in this vision standing before the Lord and the Council, with Satan himself also present to oppose him. (Zechariah 3:1.) As high priest, Joshua represented the nation before God. His garments were filthy with human excrement as he stood in for the people (also showing us Jesus defiled with the sins of the world). (Zechariah 3:3; 2 Corinthians 5:21.)

The picture is graphic and leaves no room for doubt. The nation had defiled its inheritance and was in need of restoration and recovery. The accuser was acting in the heavenly Court as the prosecutor, demanding "just punishment." God Himself rebuked Satan (v. 2), calling Joshua (representing the people — and, later, also us) a **brand plucked out of the fire.**

Then the angelic council re-dressed Joshua in glory. The changing of his garments meant the transformation of the nation as a whole (and later, the transformation of those who receive Jesus and become part of the Kingdom of God).

The angel of the Lord set before Joshua his duties. The high priest was urged to keep the way (access) to the Lord pure. (vv. 6-8.) *Way* is an access word in Scripture. Jesus, in speaking of Himself said, **I am the way, the truth, and the life** (John 14:6).

The implication for the priesthood is clear. The ways of God were to be discerned and known by the clear mandate of the Torah, and the high priest was admonished to be a custodian of the principles of life that governed the community of God, under the operation of the cloud and Council.

The angel of the Lord is concerned supremely with the house of the Lord, His sanctuary, the place of His enthronement. If the earthly place of potential enthronement is not governed by those principles essential to His coming to inhabit that house and rest there, there will be no bridge between the earthly and the heavenly.

The conferring of responsibility on Joshua to govern the spiritual service of worship in God's house and over those who served there was the highest honor — and the greatest duty or responsibility — Jehovah could bestow upon a human being.

Adam was given custodial responsibility over the Garden, and his sphere of worship was to guard the Garden from defilement and to cultivate it for the purpose of increase. (Genesis 2:15.) Had Adam, as "high priest" of the original Garden-Sanctuary been faithful in fulfilling his office, he would have had access into the heavenlies along with those birthed from his loins.

In the same fashion, Joshua, the high priest of Zechariah's day, enrobed in the splendor of God's glory as representative of the remnant nation of Judah, had the opportunity of providing a resting place for the Shekinah. This was where heaven and earth could intersect to provide the potential for an entire nation to be caught up to the throne and see things from the heavenly perspective.

God desired Zechariah, the messenger (*ma-lak* in Hebrew, literally "angel"), to show Joshua how to be a true high priest and the nation how to be a true people of the Spirit. The promise of being caught up in the Spirit was held out to Joshua provided he fulfilled his responsibility. Bear in mind this entire vision is taking place *only* for Zechariah. While he "saw" the present high priest in heaven, it was only a vision.

The angel of the Lord revealed to Zechariah his participation in the angelic council for the very purpose of enabling Joshua, and as a result the entire nation, to be brought before the throne of the Lord. The promise of access is God's desire for His people. Indeed we are told that Joshua's "companions" (lit. "men of a sign") were included in those being "given a sign" of God's future plans. (Zechariah 3:8-10.)

This strategic event in the life of Zechariah provided a point of transformation for his ministry and for his understanding of the purpose of God. The encounter with the Shekinah cloud and the sight of the Council was critical to his ability to speak for the One Who commissioned him.

One cannot speak out of what he or she has neither seen nor experienced, nor can one see or experience that to which he or she has no access. Let us now consider the free access the prophets had to the heavenly Council.

7

The Power To Ascend and Descend in Glory

The change of perspective of which we are aware as we move from Jesus to Paul . . . is a change which can be dated . . . around A.D. 30; empirically, it is a change which takes place whenever a man or woman comes to be "in Christ" . . . one's whole outlook (worldview, or paradigm of life) is revolutionized.[1]

— F. F. Bruce

To be caught up in the Spirit was to be received into the Divine Assembly, the heavenly reality within the theophanic glory-Spirit. The hallmark of the true prophet was to have stood before the Lord of glory in the midst of the deliberative Council. The false prophet had not, and consequently, lacked divine legitimation and essential qualification.

By such a vision-rapture into the heavenly presence, the prophets were raised up for missions as plenipotentiary emissaries of the Lord of Hosts, enthroned in the heavenly court. Such was the call that came to an "Isaiah" or an "Ezekiel." Introduced into the council, privileged to hear there the disclosure of the Lord's purposes, the prophets were sent to men on earth as authoritative spokesmen, as the very mouth of God.[2]

To be a man of the Spirit required an encounter in the glory cloud. As a result of being caught up, the prophet took on — or bore — the image of Lord and His likeness in glory.

The heavenly Council is the seat of origins and beginnings. The genesis of all things in the earthly arena took place in the context of the divine Council.

Here in the fullness of glory, the prophet was transformed and empowered to speak on behalf of the Council for the effecting of the divine will in the terrestrial realms. Glimpses of insight and visions of such activity are found both in the Old and New Testament. Consider for a moment the following scriptures in order to gain a greater insight into the sphere of activity that takes place in regards to the glory and access to it:

> **Now there was a day when the *sons of God*** (italics mine) **came to present themselves before the Lord, and Satan came also among them.**
>
> **Job 1:6**

> **And he dreamed, and behold a ladder set up on the earth, and the top of it reached to heaven: and behold the angels of God *ascending and descending* on it.**
>
> **Genesis 28:12**

Job is considered the oldest book in the Bible, predating Moses' writing of the Pentateuch (the first five books). It is evident that, even in ancient times, there was an awareness of angels as "sons of God," bearing the image of the glory with liberty to come and go and ascend and descend before the throne.

Also, even in the all-night wrestling match between the angel of the Lord and Jacob there came the moment of "daybreak," which implies a time of realignment in the natural and spiritual order of things, both in terms of evening and morning and in terms of ascension and descension. The angel requested release in order to ascend prior to the breaking of the day.

The issue of appearing before the Council is implied by the context of all the comparative Scriptures. (Genesis

32:26.) Each of these examples, along with many other instances, point to God's intent for His Church to ascend into glory, bear the divine image, and reveal His will in the earthly sphere of things.

If we can grasp this from the context of the life of the Savior as reported in the New Testament, it will enhance our ability to comprehend the significance of the matter. Of the four gospels, John is the one replete with symbol and metaphor.

It is the "gospel of the Eagle," that heavenly awareness of the Eternal One, Who, though lofty, exalted and pre-existent, comes to make His abode in man's domain. The early Church fathers viewed the four faces of the winged creatures in Revelation 4:7 as indications of the four-fold profile of the Son of God as revealed metaphorically in the gospels.

Therefore, the Anti-Nicene fathers saw the Lion of Judah (the *true* Lion-King) revealed in Matthew, the ox or servant face revealed in Mark, the face of the Son of Man revealed in Luke, and the face of the Eternal Eagle-Son of God revealed in John.

Eugene Peterson put it this way in translating John 1:14: "The Word became flesh and blood, and moved into the neighborhood."[3]

The issue of ascending and descending appears early in John's account. We are told in John 1 that Philip, who was from Bethsaida, found Nathaniel and invited him to discover for himself that Jesus was the One spoken of in the Law and the Prophets as Messiah.

Nathaniel had great difficulty believing that Messiah could come from Nazareth, a lowly place in the former territory of the northern nation of Israel (the ten tribes), as Scripture declared Messiah would be from Bethlehem, the heart of Judah and birthplace of King David. Nathaniel responded with an honest skepticism that was actually praised by Jesus. This gave him a level of credibility allowing him to have a quite revealing encounter with the Master. (John 1:44-51, esp. vv. 46-48.)

Teachers of the Torah would sit under a fig tree while teaching the scriptures, so there is an allusion to the fact that Nathaniel was both a teacher and a student of the Torah, who was seeking diligently for the keys to the arrival of Messiah. The Master's insight into the "guileless" character of this honest skeptic led to Nathaniel's confession of Jesus as Son of God.

Jesus Is the "Ladder"

The response of Jesus was so powerful and revealing that it unlocks the mystery of the incident of "Jacob's ladder." Also, Nathaniel's confession of Jesus as Son of God and King of Israel was far greater than a recognition of His Messianic role.

Jesus is not just the One spoken of in the Law of Moses and all the Prophets, He is also the Word of God, Eternal and Omnipotent, Who was enthroned above the cherubim in kingly glory and splendor. He is the One through Whom all creation was manifested and by Whom all prophetic dialogue took place!

Based on his confession, which was as powerful as the confession of Peter in Caesarea Philippi (Matthew 16:16), Nathaniel was promised that he would see the heavens opened. There was to be for him a rending of the veil between earth and heaven. He was to see into the divine glory-Council in a fuller sense now that Jesus was present as the incarnate Son of Man, a deliberate reference to Daniel 7 and the concept of the divine Son of Man.

Jesus was declaring that He *is* Jacob's ladder. Angelic glory ascends and descends upon Him. For the Church to be "caught up" into the Council, it no longer needs a "rapture" into the glory cloud to authorize her to speak on God's behalf. The transitional point, the very pivotal point, has been reached in Christ.

He *is* the ladder, He is the access into the throne room. The unveiling of the truth about the Son of Man, the testimony of Jesus, is, as we have already stated, the "spirit of prophecy." There is no other "Way" into the Father's presence and the glory. Furthermore, Jesus is the very House of God Himself. Jesus, the STONE with OIL poured on it where heaven and earth meet, is our "Bethel." (Genesis 28:19.) Jacob, a type of the believer, witnessed to the sanctity of the *place*, anointed it, and made it an altar.

Nathaniel, by his confession, anointed Jesus Head over his own life. His confession gave Jesus the opportunity to open heaven to Nathaniel and make the higher realm of glory accessible in the lower realm of humanity.

For Jacob, the *place* was awesome, for it provided a gateway to access the divine Council. (Genesis 28:16,17.) He had stumbled on what appeared to be an ordinary stone, and made it his pillow, not knowing the Lord was there. The rabbis believed that place was where Abraham built the altar to slay Isaac on Mount Moriah, hence it was "destiny" for Jacob to stumble upon it.[4]

Jesus is the STONE, cut out of the mountain without hands (Daniel 2:35,45), which Nathaniel did not realize he had stumbled upon. But in stumbling over it, the STONE indeed broke him open, whereby the heavenly glory was opened to him. He saw that Christ *is* that very gate! (Matthew 21:44; Luke 20:18.)

The gate is no longer a place, as it was for Jacob. The gate is a Person, Who is not merely the access point between heaven and earth, but the very presence of the glory come near to us to make true worship possible.

The gate is Jesus, Who provides opportunity to ascend into the cloud on an ongoing basis. It is not temple-centered or mountain-centered worship that now pleases the Father. (John 4:21-24.) Person-centered worship in the glory Spirit, and the truth of the Man Himself as the revelation of God in the earth, is that in which the Father finds pleasure.

God and man are perfectly at one in Christ. He is the very locus of divine revelation and the express image of the glory. For the believer, prophetic revelation and insight into the Council will be dynamically realized in a progressive unveiling.

Every picture of ascension and descension finds its ultimate expression in God's Man, Christ Jesus. He is the apex of truth, the *telos* (the *end*) of the law unto righteousness (Romans 10:4), the glory Moses had to hide for the people could not bear to look at the image of God on a man.

> **But if the ministration of death, written and engraven in stones, was glorious, so that the children of Israel could not stedfastly behold the face of Moses for the glory of his countenance;** *which glory was to be done away* (or was to pass away when Jesus came.)
>
> **2 Corinthians 3:7**

Telos, translated "to be done away with" in the verse above, refers to "a definite point or goal . . . the point aimed at as the limit . . . to (the) conclusion of an act or state . . . the ultimate."[5]

The sons of Israel could not stand to look at the "ultimate aim of the law, the goal of the law, the zenith or high point of the law, the *end* of the law." What the Israelites rejected was the opportunity to ascend into the glory, behold the image of God, and stand in the Council of Jehovah.

Under the New Covenant, we have been given unlimited access to ascend into the glory at any given moment in Christ. In 2 Corinthians 3:18, Paul made it clear that the immediacy of access and ascension is ever available to the believer.

Insight into the mind and purpose of God is our birthright in the New Covenant. Our difficulty is not lack of access, but the modern rationalistic worldview in which even Christians are steeped from birth. We have become desensitized to the invisible reality of the Kingdom of God; therefore, we suffer from spiritual "sensory deprivation."

The nature of prophetic ministry in the New Covenant is clearly tied to healing a people of their lack of sensitivity in order to help them behold the glory of God and to gain insight into the mind and purpose of God.

Prophetic ministry is to help the children of God become transformed to bear His image, be *sent* out of the Council chambers, and *descend* into the lives of both believers and non-believers who have fallen short of the glory and provide them an example of life in Christ in the context of glory.

There can never be dynamic speech to change events of history for the purpose of God, unless there is a fresh "seeing" of the glory in Christ. All prophetic speech rises out of a progressive apprehension of Christ as temple and presence of God. To be "in the Spirit" is to be in the process of becoming the intention of God[6] and bearing the image of the glory.

Attentiveness and sensitivity to the Spirit provides us with moments of "ascension," where we can rise above things in our perceptions and circumstances. That enables us to see and hear things from a heavenly perspective which enables and empowers us both to be transformed and to become agents of transformation in the course of our day-to-day existence.

The Ordination of Jesus

One final comment on this matter of ascending and descending would be in order. In the twilight discourse between Nicodemus and Jesus (John 3:12,13), the confused rabbi has no comprehension whatsoever of Jesus' comment on ascension and descension. Jesus was not referring to His future ascension, but rather a present and active qualifying for His prophetic role as Messiah.

Jesus, in the tradition of Isaiah, Ezekiel, and the other prophets, declared His validity as a true prophet by having been caught up into the Council and thus seeing into the glory. According to the gospels, this happened in His thirtieth year. (Luke 3:21-23.) That was the prophet's age when the glory appeared to Him and He saw into the heavens. Then he was empowered to speak on behalf of the divine intention. (Ezekiel 1:1.)

We know from the law of Moses, that at thirty years of age, priests were ordained into active service, although their lives prior to that time had been spent in preparation. The anointing of the priest typified the overshadowing of the glory and the authorization of the divine Council by the hand of Moses. (Numbers 4:3,23,30,35,39,43,47.)

The prophet, however, had to have seen into the very glory and been in the Council itself. Moses must ascend the mountain and be caught up into the glory in order to see a pattern intended to be reproduced. (Exodus 24:15-18.) Even so, in fulfillment of the Law and the Prophets, Jesus must ascend into the glory and behold the image there, then be *sent* from there by decree, just as Isaiah had to be sent. (Isaiah 6:8.)

For Jesus, however, it was not to hear the question, "Whom shall I send?" Rather, what Jesus heard was, "This is My Beloved Son." (Matthew 3:17; Mark 1:11; Luke 3:22.)

In **the fulness of time** (Galatians 4:4), the ultimate purpose was made manifest. God had not merely *sent* a prophet, but *given* a Son. Jesus, the very Son of God, was not only sent from the glory, but given for Nicodemus — and for the whole world.[7] (John 3:11,17.)

8

The Voice That Can Be Missed

Only the Roman government was more powerful in Palestine than the organized and dreaded Pharisees . . . They placed extreme emphasis on the question of the external rather than the internal . . . They had made up their minds early that (Jesus) was not the Christ or any other of God's relatives! . . . Christ and the Pharisees hit head on with a bang comparable to two cars colliding on the highway.[1]

— William L. Coleman

Nicodemus, a wealthy "ruler of the Jews," was intrigued enough to make a clandestine visit to Jesus by night, as we saw in the last chapter. (John 3:1-21.) Of all the Pharisees, he at least recognized that Jesus was sent from God because of the miracles He had done. Only one other of the ruling group, which protected its paradigm even to murder, ever believed on Jesus. That was Joseph of Arimathea. (Matthew 27:57.)

It is obvious that Nicodemus wrestled with recognition of Jesus as the One of whom the prophets had spoken. Later, in the Sanhedrin, when he mildly defended Jesus (John 7:51), he was accused of being "a Galilean," meant as an insult.

William Coleman has written that Nicodemus' defense was similar to a man standing on a track to stop a train: "Except for the faintest thud, the project went on without interruption."[2]

The Pharisees by that time had become so arrogant and so protective of their "turf" that they read the words of Isaiah, Jeremiah, and Ezekiel, but would have killed them also if they had appeared in Jerusalem declaiming the very same words.

The ancient prophets spoke out of an all-consuming vision. They saw the glory, and all their prophesying was tied to what they saw, not to what then *was*. The issue of vision is *seeing*, the issue of seeing is *specificity*!

The problem was that the leaders of Jesus' day had lost that all-consuming vision of the glory. Clouding their minds was a "vision" of a scenario constructed by the rabbis during the past century or so. This scenario had built an expectation of two Messiahs: one who would "suffer" for the sins of the people and one who would "ride a white horse" and lead the Jews to victory over the Romans and, then, the entire world.

Baker's *Encyclopedia of the Bible* says:

> . . . It is highly doubtful that anyone imagined the Messiah would accomplish His salvational work by means of His own death (cf. Isaiah 53:12). When rabbinic speculation failed to satisfactorily harmonize the paradoxical facts of humiliation and exaltation, some hypothesized that God would send a Messiah to suffer as well as a Messiah to reign.[3]

Jesus somehow did not fit into the picture of either "messiah," which is the danger of constructing preconceived ideas of what God is going to do. The prophetic ministry is to find out from God what He intends to do, not build a scenario on man's ideas of what He might do.

Even in the New Testament, Paul described his calling as based on vision. He declared that he was not disobedient to the *heavenly vision*. (Acts 26:19.) It was his *seeing* that led to his speaking. *Vision has a voice!* There is a prophetic declaration that arises out of the visionary experience. Without the voice there is no way for hearers to discern what the Spirit is endeavoring to accomplish. (Revelation 2:7,17,29, 3:6,13,22.)

In Pisidian Antioch, Paul entered the synagogue on the Sabbath and, following the customary reading of the Law and the Prophets, he requested permission to exhort the worshippers. In the course of his preaching he made a very potent statement:

> **For they that dwell at Jerusalem, and their rulers, because they knew him not, nor yet the voices of the prophets which are read every sabbath day, they have fulfilled them in condemning him.**
>
> **Acts 13:27**

Paul made it abundantly evident that the sin of reductionism was all too prevalent in Jewish worship. The *voices of the prophets* had been reduced by the nations of Israel and Judah. After years of ritual and routine, the Israelites lost sight of the purpose of the Sabbath and lost the ability to hear the voices of the prophets.

The Jewish teachers of the law and the Pharisees of Jesus' day could clearly quote the *words* of the prophets, but the *voices* were not heard at all. They did the very opposite of what the prophets spoke or intended: They crucified the Lord of glory. The One Who was to sit enthroned as Finisher of the work was cursed and crucified. He was the "Alpha," but they refused to accept Him as the "Omega." They missed the voices of the prophets.

The prophets had no doubt at all as to what they saw, and they spoke out of what they saw. They were focused, intentional, and declarative. Their eye was "single" and thus the body of the vision they communicated was full of light. (Matthew 6:22.)

As we see over and over in the gospels, every seventh day, the words of the prophets were read, as what we know as the Old Testament was discussed a section at a time. The rhythm of the weekly celebration of the Sabbath was held in awe and wonder. However, the Pharisees never understood the purpose of the Sabbath where it concerned the glory and image of God.

The Glory in the Sabbath

The Sabbath was designed by God to be a focus of reminder of Him and His glory, as well as of His purpose in creating man. Over a period of six days, there came a proceeding and progressive word from the Shekinah until there was finality. The Spirit of glory hovered continually for the six-day period until the earth bore the image of the sanctuary of God. Deity completed all things and declared them "very good" at the end of the sixth day. (Genesis 1:31.)

There was a forming and shaping that unfolded out of the brooding presence and creative Word until, on the seventh day, there was a *resting* of the glory cloud over the created order. In other words, there was an enthronement of the glory on the finished work. The Sabbath was set apart and hallowed because it marked the finishing of God's creative work. He blessed the seventh day and made it holier than the rest. (Genesis 2:1-3.)

God has every intention of occupying what He created to be His inter-galactic temple. Heaven is His throne, and the earth is His footstool. (Isaiah 66:1.) A "footstool" is for the *resting* of the feet of one who is seated. The King enthroned in glory yet broods over the "chaos" to recover His image in the earthly arena. He intends to ultimately rest His feet on something worthy of His name and glory.

Even David comprehended the prophetic significance of Sabbath glory when he intended to build a house of rest for the Ark of the Testimony and as God's footstool. (1 Chronicles 28:2.) In the musical, *We Are Called*, by Stephen Fry, David is quoted from Psalm 132, in Fry's powerful song "Oh, the Glory of Your Presence":

> "So arise from Your *REST*, and be blessed by our praise,
>   as we glory in Your embrace,
>   as Your presence now fills this place."

David declared it in this manner in Psalm 132:8:

Arise, O Lord, into thy *rest* (resting place); thou, and the ark of thy strength.

The word for "resting place" in that verse is the Hebrew word for enthronement, the concept of Sabbath in Genesis. While the term used is *menuhah*, it is the verbal root for rest.[4]

The picture points prophetically to the final *day of the Lord* when He will reign uncontested over all His works and His people will fully enter His enthronement glory. This is indeed what the prophets anticipated and saw, and of what they spoke. Theirs was to be a *voice* from the throne.

The tragedy, however, is that those who continually — week after week, month after month, and year after year — heard the words of the prophets lost their ability to hear the voice of the prophets and forfeited a right to access what the prophet saw. Modernity has done much the same to the Church. The weekly rhythm of Sabbath glory has been reduced to routine and ritual for many church-goers. Their routine has not led to a renewal. They have become "dull of hearing." (Hebrews 5:11.)

There are prophetically many things concerning Him which must be spoken, but if we have reduced things to words and routines, the voices of the prophets will again be missed in the Church in our generation. Preoccupation with methodologies and mechanisms to "guarantee" ministry success can blur the vision of heavenly glory. This hinders us from hearing the *voices of the prophets* and causes us to despise prophesying. (1 Thessalonians 5:20.)

Tragically, the issue of "despising the prophetic" is often due to the abuse of the operation of the prophetic utterance. There are immature and unstable people who offer "a word from the Lord" that obviously is not. However, we ought not let their misuse or mistakes keep us from recognizing the true prophetic.

Much of what the prophets of old declared is yet being fulfilled in Christ and the Church. There is nothing left to be revealed, but much left to be illumined. One of the issues we need to carefully consider and guard against is the idea of what is called in some circles "revelation knowledge."

God has, once and for all, spoken to us in His Son, Whom He made heir of all things, and through Whom He made the entire cosmos. (Hebrews 1:1-3.) There will never be any other revelation given to anyone. The revelation is complete in Christ. The Scripture is complete from Genesis to Revelation.

To claim "revelation knowledge" is to speak beyond the completed revelation already given in the Son. However, we do not want to fall into the error of those who reduce the Word to something in the past void of any power for the present. We need to understand that, while all the revelation we will ever need has been given, all of it has not yet been *illumined* to us!

It is not revelation we need, but illumination on the *completed* revelation of the Son. The voices of the prophets can still be missed if, like the Pharisees, we exchange Him for some theological "hobby-horse." We must be careful not to fall into polemical arguments about particular "convictions" regarding any number of relatively minor issues. This only leads to division and strife, not illuminated revelation.

Can the Church Become Like the Pharisees?

The Church is to be a "seeing and hearing" company. When we fail to "see and hear," we lose our prophetic edge (our "salt-ness," Matthew 5:13), and are not fit even to be trampled underfoot by the world. The ultimate intention for which God patiently constructed the descendants of Abraham into a nation was not fulfilled in them.

First Israel, and then Judah, fell short of God's purpose to bless all the families of the earth through the Israelites. (Genesis 12:1-3.) The remnant of the Jews who returned from Babylonian exile had prospered and multiplied in the land, but they also had became exclusive, sectarian, selfish, and ingrown.

Most of the wealthy and "royal" descendants of David and of the genealogically accredited families (Ezra 2; Nehemiah 7:6-63) still lived at the very center of the nation, in the place where glory was to be enthroned: Jerusalem. Jesus came from the royal line but of a family of comparatively "poor relations," living in the now-contaminated territory that once had been the northern nation of Israel.

However, close proximity to the temple, worship, and the reading of the Scriptures actually caused the learned and well-to-do Jews to take those things for granted. They lost the sense of reverence for the presence of glory. Sabbath was no longer a day to expect glory but a routine to be followed.

They had become controllers of the Sabbath, until there was no glory at all, only legalism. They took the prophets and twisted their words, because they lost the ability to hear their voices. They were no longer able to hear *the voices of the prophets* because they had lost the vision of the true desire of God for Sabbath, which was "glory enthronement."

The revelation of the prophets in Scripture was missed to the point where those who lived in Jerusalem actually crucified and killed the very Lord of the Sabbath. Likewise, is it possible for the Church to lapse into spiritual blindness and deafness while quoting Scripture?

Is it possible that the Church may *kill* any fresh movement of the Spirit of God? Sadly enough, it is not only possible, but inevitable — *if we do not maintain the vision of the glory*. The exact same situation has occurred over and over down through the history of Old Testament times and throughout the past two millenia.

The Spirit of God is working to recover for Christ, and in Christ, all that the prophets saw and declared as the intention of the Father. (Acts 3:21-26.)

The challenge for us is to overcome the tendency to reduce God to predictability, contradicting the very notion of the freedom of God. To miss the "voice of the prophets" is to domesticate them to fit a man-made program and agenda. All "domesticated" things are, by definition, "tamed" and subject to rule and labor.

To domesticate the prophets is to miss their voice. They cry from outside the environs of Jerusalem. They are never easily assimilated into the courts of kings for their voice is an irritating one. They speak about things of which Sabbath-controllers want no part.

When the voices of the prophets cannot be heard, it is because the leaders and/or the people do not *want* to hear. Issues of justice and compassion are not popular when survival of man-made kingdoms are at stake.

If those who "dwell in Jerusalem" can domesticate the prophets until others think the real meaning of Sabbath is the right of leaders to control others, than the end will be the crucifying afresh of the Son of God. *The end of all domestication is control.*

The Word of the Lord is the voice of the Lord.

The voice of the Lord is the VOICE of the prophets.

If indeed there has been an apprehending of the glory in Christ and an ascending into Him, the prophets will give Him VOICE in their message. The Lord of glory is not One to cater to the whims of man nor the dictates of society.

The voices of the prophets can be missed because the VOICE of the Lord is disregarded. To disregard the voice of the Lord is to do so at our own peril. When systems of government and church communities fail to give heed to the voices of the prophets, they have lost the focus of the prophetic intention. The end result has been the domestication (control) of the words of the prophets, from Abraham to John the Baptist.

Reducing the Prophetic Word Brings Death

The reduction of their words has always led to the marginalizing of the Christ, until His desire is no longer even considered. His words become mere platitudes for social reform and political ambition, and the life goes out of them.

Deity then becomes subject to "de-mythologizing" and slander by the theological courts of the cursed and the damned. Jesus becomes a specimen out of history with which scoffers and mockers rush to find fault.

The farther humanity moves from Him, the more they think they can find fault with Him. In the first century, those of the world who examined Him closely in full view and clear vision could find no fault in Him. (John 19:4; Luke 23:4.) Those of His own people, who already had "killed" (Matthew 23:37) the voice of the prophets and wanted to accuse Him, had to acquire false testimony in order to destroy Him. (Matthew 26:59,60.)

The religious debaters of this age have felt justified in destroying the notion of the freedom of God by not giving heed to the voices of the prophets. It remains to be seen what the ultimate outcome of all the arguing and debating from those of the school of higher criticism to the doctrinal wrangling of denominations — will be.

The Church needs an awakened ear once again to the voices of the prophets, who saw an all-comprehensive vision of the purpose of God in Christ. It is a necessity that we do not fail to walk in the power of the Spirit and "kiss the Son" (Psalm 2:12), lest we too find ourselves judged with the unbelieving world and find destruction at the portals of our places of worship. (Acts 3:23.)

The ultimate Prophet Himself agonized over the deafness of the nation and reiterated the agony of David, Jeremiah, and Isaiah (Psalm 116:19, 122:2, 137:5, 147:12; Isaiah 40:9, 51:17, 52:1,2; Jeremiah 4:14, 6:8, 7:29, 13:27, 15:5), when He cried:

O Jerusalem, Jerusalem, thou that killest the prophets, and stonest them which are sent unto thee,

how often would I have gathered thy children together, even as a hen gathereth her chickens under her wings, and ye would not!

Behold, your house is left unto you *desolate*.

Matthew 23:37,38

Once we "domesticate" the prophets' words, we have lost the vision they saw and cannot any longer hear the voice out of which they spoke. The only thing that remains is the structure of the house, but no substantive glory is finding any *rest* there. There is no Sabbath in a *desolate* house, which is a "haunted" place. Eliminating the voices of the prophets leaves only the howling of demonizing spirits to be heard, seeking a place of habitation.

If glory departs, the demonic will quickly move in to satisfy its own perverse need for worship, while deceiving those who give it such. In the end, those who domesticated the voice of the prophets will themselves be domesticated by a systematized evil and driven by demonic influence. (Isaiah 34:8-17, especially v. 11.)

The sad result of being left desolate is that the last estate is "worse than the first." The ousted demon returns with seven others stronger than himself. Jesus' teaching on those who come to God, yet do not fill the cleansed "house" with His glory, was in the specific context of addressing the leaders of His day, whom He called an "evil generation." (Matthew 12:39,45.)

By that, he meant the scribes, Pharisees, and religious rulers who kept the people in darkness. They had made the revealed Word of God of no avail. They would not keep it and would not let the people keep it. (Matthew 23:1-39, esp. v. 13.)

His warning could just as well be aimed at much of religious liberalism today, as well as to evangelicalism that claims "a form of godliness but denies the power thereof." (2 Timothy 3:5.) Any generation that teaches the "doctrines of men" in place of the commandments of God is in danger of judgment. (Matthew 15:8,9.)In his study of the Pharisees, Coleman also wrote:

> The Pharisees are not-too-distant cousins. They have done very little that we have not worked hard to match in action or in spirit. We have used them as "whipping-posts" when, in fact, they make better mirrors. . . .[5]

We can miss the *voice* of the prophets as easily as did the Pharisees, if we do not make sure the paradigm by which we live is God's paradigm shared by true prophets.

9

Making a Way Out of No Way

> Therefore we see that to us nothing is promised to be expected from the Lord, which we are not also bidden to ask of Him in prayers. So true is it that we dig up by prayer the treasures that were pointed out by the Lord's gospel, and which our faith has gazed upon.[1]
>
> — John Calvin

Issues of exodus are important issues for the people of God. The flow of biblical history is replete with accounts of God working through prophetic vessels to "make a way out of no way." The dynamic of such history-making events is tied to a travail and a cry that precipitates a release for the nation or sometimes for individuals.

This cycle in the life of the Israelites is repeated again and again in the book of Judges. They would fail to obey God, become oppressed by other nations, and "cry out" in repentance. God then would raise up a judge to bring about an "exodus" event, providing the people with a way out of no way.

The most well-known model for "a way out of no way" is found in the early part of the book of Exodus. Our understanding of prophetic paradigms (models or worldviews) requires an adequate comprehension of the seasons in which God moves to restore and recover what is lost.

And it came to pass in the process of time, that the king of Egypt died: and the children of Israel

sighed (groaned) by reason of the bondage, and they cried, and their cry came up (arose) unto God by reason of the bondage.

And God heard their groaning, and God remembered his covenant with Abraham, with Isaac, and with Jacob.

And God *looked upon* the children of Israel, and God had respect (acknowledged) unto them.

Exodus 2:23-25

The cry of the children of Israel was born out of the necessity of survival and, whether they realized it or not, a need for the renewing of their identity as a people. Survival modes will shape our speech in the presence of God in a way that other modes of existence will not.

If things are well, and there is no worry about survival, our speech will not be one of desperation. Our words are shaped by the context of circumstances in which we find ourselves. The struggle for the Israelites was that they carried a corporate consciousness of being the elect of God, only to experience life in bondage.

There was indeed a contradiction between who they believed they were and where they found themselves circumstantially. How can the elect of God be in bondage? Their groaning was born out of the internal contradiction that tormented them day and night.

The bricks may not have been as hard to deal with as was the inner awareness that they were the seed of Abraham and had been promised to be heirs of the world. After years of hard slave labor and endurance, some may even have thought the promise of becoming an heir was an illusion perpetuated by an ancestor who lived in another day and time.

Perhaps, they thought it was time to lay aside "false beliefs" that God indeed would bring them out of bondage. Yet the toil and labor of the brickyard only intensified their groaning. The worse things became, the more internal contradiction they felt.

The crying out that took place does not even indicate that they cried out to God specifically. The text merely indicates that they cried out, and that *because of desperation engendered by the oppression of bondage,* their cry had the power to get the attention of God and put Him into a remembrance mode.

God Who never forgets does, however, have the power to remember. In hearing their groaning, He determined to send them a prophet to deliver them. He chose a man named Moses through whom to work an "exodus event." Moses was to "make a way out of no way."

An extremely important lesson for us — one which we often overlook in the story of the exodus — is the indication that had the children of Israel not cried out, God would not have sent them a deliverer!

John Wesley commented that it seems God has set up perimeters for His children so that, unless someone prays (intercedes, beseeches, asks, and keeps on asking — Matthew 7:7,8), God does not move.[2]

The late E. M. Bounds, one of the greatest writers on prayer of our time, said:

> Prayer is the one prime, eternal condition by which the Father is pledged to put the Son in possession of the world. Christ prays through His people. . . . We are not praying after the order that moves God and brings all divine influences to help us. . . . We do not pray as Elijah prayed.[3]

That does not mean God cannot move without prayer, but only that His purpose for creating those in His image is to have children who will work in "cooperation" with Him. On those occasions when His will is to do something or to show mercy, He will find those to ask Him to do it, as with Abraham and the destruction of Sodom and Gomorrah. (Genesis 18:18-33.)

The problem there was that Abraham did not go far enough. He stopped when he reached the number of ten believers in the town for which God would spare the area. Too many times, even today, we do not go "far enough" in our prayers.

God Responds to Our Cries

The prophetic call of Moses hinged upon God having heard the cry of the people and remembering His covenant with their fathers.

> **Now therefore, behold, the cry of the children of Israel is come unto me: and I have also seen the oppression wherewith the Egyptians oppress them.**
>
> **Come now therefore, and I will send thee unto Pharaoh, that thou mayest bring forth my people the children of Israel out of Egypt.**
>
> **Exodus 3:9,10**

The people of Israel were fighting for their future. They needed to survive. Their need shaped their reality and their speech. They cried out, and Jehovah responded in the affirmative. The cry arose because of their bondage. (Exodus 2:24.)

Their identity provided a point of support for their faith; their extremity was that they were under the weight of Egyptian bondage. Between their identity in the midst of crisis and their extremity under the bondage of crisis, faith found a point of leverage.

Thus, we might say that *faith* began to form a weapon on the opposite end of where they were and bore down on their souls until it pushed the weight of bondage so high that it got the attention of Jehovah:

• The cry was at the opposite end of their extremity.

• The cry was the voice of incongruence between who they were and where they found themselves.

• The cry was a people intuitively asking for an "exodus event."

• The cry was their faith manifesting as a groan.

• The cry was a voiceless plea for deliverance more than a confession of confidence.

However, the weight of the oppression provided the opportunity for little Israel to overthrow big Egypt. Prophetic ministry responds to bring in the new thing, once the old thing has caused us to groan. It is not that we have eyes for the new thing, it is merely that the old thing has become too heavy to bear, thus providing an opportunity for groaning.

There are seasons in the life of the Church in various places, when Christians have lost sight of what the future can indeed hold in terms of promise for the elect. Yet our groans provide God with a point of leverage between who we truly are and what we are suffering under, for deliverance to occur by an in-breaking of new truth! (Romans 8:22-28.)

There are exodus events that cannot occur and prophetic declarations that cannot be made, until there is a groan and a travail that rises out of the depths of the elect. We must truly "hunger and thirst" in desperation before we can be filled to satiation. (Matthew 5:6.)

Somehow, because of our humanness, real transformational change cannot take place unless there are crisis points to provide leverage for our pathos and God's power. Between our pressure and God's power lies the pivotal point for prophetic intervention. This intervention begins by delivering us from worn-out paradigms and then brings us into divine patterns of progressive access to ascending glory.

The call of Moses was born out of the groan of a people whose humanity had been diminished in a flurry of quotas. The demand to meet quotas diminishes our ability to be wholly ourselves. We can find ourselves in the desperate place of being driven to accomplish more, get more, find more, and do more. All the while, we are becoming less human and increasingly automatic in our reactions and responses to the daily issues of life.

To regain or maintain our wholeness demands an exodus. The model of Moses as a pattern for prophetic ministry is worth considering insofar as God intends to shape our understanding by his example. We have already seen that God promised to raise up a prophet like Moses from among the people. (Deuteronomy 18:15.)

The Apostle Peter referred to Christ as this promised prophet in the context of his sermon following the healing of the lame man at the Gate Beautiful. (Acts 3:22.)

Prophets Speak Forth Possibilities

The prophetic model found in Moses is that of first a *deliverer* and then what I would call a *visionary-builder*. His ministry of deliverance provided the impetus for the exodus event that brought the people out of the brick-yard once and for all. They then crossed over a veritable "sea" *as though* it were not a sea at all. (Exodus 14:22-27; Hebrews 11:29.)

Moses, as the prophet of God, created a passageway where none existed. He allowed something to become possible that was outside the realm of possibility. The foundation of genuine prophetic motivation is the power to energize the faith of a people to follow God into a dead end, only to discover that the dead end is actually an open end.

We must be careful not to presume that there is some manipulation of circumstances or of the Almighty by the prophet in this context. This could not be farther from the truth. For this reason, all who speak on behalf of God need guidelines that enable them to walk in a context of accountability. The danger is that they cross the line of demarcation and find themselves in a realm of manipulation and divination.

Also, this principle does not merely apply to those who are prophetically motivated. It has become popular to slander any who are referred to in any dimension as prophetic. It would do all ministers of the Gospel well to realize that whether we be pastors, evangelists, teachers, apostles or prophets, we are called to lead by a word proceeding from God. (Deuteronomy 8:3.)

We are all called to prefer one another in love and are required to have ears to hear what the Spirit is saying to the Church. The overarching dimension of prophetic motivation is foundational for all that God is about in His Church. (Ephesians 2:20.)

The Mosaic paradigm began, as previously stated, in a work of deliverance. The ten plagues were ten progressive releases of the power of God to dismantle and de-legitimize the claims of Egypt on the elect of God. In obedience to God, Moses began with the least-significant principality in Egyptian worship and progressively dismantled the power-base undergirding the fountain-head of all the Egyptian deities.[4] (Exodus 8-11.)

When the Israelites finally were allowed to leave, the Egyptians were left bereft of an entire slave population, of the next generation that would have ensued from all of the firstborn sons, and of gods on whose power they could count. Thus, they were left without an immediate future.

Prophetic ministry must, by the demonstration of the Spirit and power, de-legitimize the claims of the powers of injustice on the people we serve in the five-fold ministry. This is the only way in which famine and poverty, racism and exploitation, oppression and greed will no longer be able to diminish the humanness of the elect of God.

It is not that we ought to transform water into blood, or dirt into gnats, or multiply frogs in our backyards. It is rather that we must find the power of the Spirit to engage us in present issues that have the potential of being transformed by the same Spirit. We can apply the lessons of the ageless story of the Exodus to the current age.

There is a desperate need for the restoration of prophetic preaching in the land. It is the "foolishness of preaching" that must regain a primacy in the world. (1 Corinthians 1:21.) Preaching by men and women with prophetic conviction, who are not ashamed of the cross, indeed is the power of God that will issue forth in salvation. (1 Corinthians 1:18.)

There is power available in the Spirit, if we will be seized by that Spirit. Then we must lay hold of the ancient text and let Christ be the hermeneutic from which we preach. We must speak as it were, the oracles of God (1 Peter 4:11). Then we can watch as God confirms His Word with signs and wonders in our day even as He did in days past. (Hebrews 2:3,4.)

Let our brothers who scoff at the miraculous and claim it was for a bygone era continue to scoff, but let those "who have ears to hear what the Spirit says to the Church," be impressed upon to preach the only message to which God is committed to bear witness. If we do this, the world will see a great outpouring of the Spirit with signs and wonders following. (Mark 16:15-18.)

There are yet powers and principalities that need to be challenged and overthrown, and there are yet many who love God but remain enslaved in areas of their lives. There must come a groundswell of groaning from deep within the Church of the Lord Jesus. We must travail in hope for greater exodus events in the overall scheme of things before God can truly restore a prophetic anointing in the Church for the matter of recovery.

Salvation: the Greatest Paradigm for Exodus

Eugene Peterson tells us that both the Greek and Hebrew words for *salvation* carry the connotation of "being set free from a cramped existence."[5]

The preaching of the cross (which is the paradigm for the greatest of all exodus events) provides the Spirit the opportunity to work in the hearer a leverage point between his or her bondage and potential and to bring freedom from a cramped existence.

The preaching of the cross provides God with an opportunity to "make a way out of no way" for those who are "foolish" enough to believe that He indeed is God. The foolishness of God is worth the risk.

There is a groan being heard in many "brickyards" in today's society. There are the trappings of the post-modern era that are diminishing the humanness of many of the peoples of the world. Racial issues, gender issues, and class issues are more volatile than ever before.

The desperation in the generations growing up is evident in the high rate of teen suicide, increasing chemical abuse, violence, and sexual misconduct. For all our learning and education, our systems are failing. It seems as though the frogs are multiplying, and society cannot get rid of them.

The genocide of the unborn is at such an alarming high that only at two other periods in the history of the world has there been known such a travesty of justice and righteousness. In both previous instances, the powers and principalities worked within the established systems to destroy the coming generation. In both instances, however, there was a prophetic voice protected through wise and God-fearing servants of Yahweh.

Both Moses and Jesus were supernaturally protected in order that they might be *raised up* out of the presence of a death sentence on their generation to work an exodus event in the appropriate season.

It behooves us to consider again the presence of an Unseen Hand at work to *raise up* a generation of prophetically motivated believers who will learn how to cooperate with the Lord of glory in this day to "make a way out of no way." There seems to be a numbing and false belief that exodus events are a thing of the past. This could not be farther from the truth.

Exodus events are a thing of the future, and in fact, are the only way into the future. As the Spirit of God can help the Church to apprehend the greater purpose for prophetic ministry, we will begin to hear of breakthroughs and passageways in the lives of many who were stopped at a dead end called "No Exit."

10

The Resting Place of the Glory

Glory is what we all lost when we lost touch with God. Glory is what we seek — the recovery of that loss. . . . God is ready to pour His glory upon us, purge us with its fire, overflow us with its power and bring us to His created purpose for our lives.[1]

— Jack Hayford

Exodus events are essential to freedom, but freedom without structure is anarchy. Freedom is for a purpose. Paul told us that it was for freedom that Christ set us free. (Galatians 5:1.) Issues of slavery and freedom for Paul were tied to issues of justification by faith. Justification by faith is directly in relationship to obedience to God. (Romans 1:5.) Faith, to be biblical faith, expresses itself in obedience to God.

Moses (a paradigm for the prophetic ministry of Jesus) worked an exodus event as a *deliverer*. However, he also led the people to the Mountain of God, where he revealed a pattern that he had seen. (Exodus 25:9.) In turn, Moses was responsible for overseeing the construction of that pattern until it was able to house the very glory-presence of God. (Exodus 40:33-35.)

Moses himself bore the image of the glory, as we have already seen. In the instructions for the building of the tabernacle and all the furnishings, he mediated that same Spirit both to the structure itself and to the Aaronic priesthood by anointing both with the holy anointing oil. (Exodus 30:22-30.)

97

The anointing with oil served to both prepare and symbolize the descent of the glory cloud upon the structure and the priesthood, so that the house was filled with the glory. In the anointing of the priesthood, there also was a need to anoint the garments of the high priest.

The anointing of Aaron's garments serve as a type of the investiture of man with the image of the glory enthroned above the Cherubim. Adam's transgression led to his nakedness. His nakedness was a result of the loss of the image of glory. (Genesis 3:10.)

It is worth noting that the word for "naked" in the Hebrew is the same root word for *subtle*. In Genesis 3:1, we are told that the serpent was more "subtle" or "crafty" than any other beast of the field which the Lord God had made.

Jehovah was really querying Adam about his image and character when he asked, "Who told you that you were *naked*?" The text could just as easily read: Who told you that you were crafty?

The reason this is significant is because it expresses the fact that Adam exchanged the glory image of the Creator for the image of a creature, became corrupted (Romans 1:23) and behaved like a "crawling creature." This is not unlike the picture we see of the woman who was "bowed low" for eighteen years by satanic device. (Luke 13:16.)

As Satan is typified by a crawling creature that is low to the ground, then in order to behold him, one must "bow low." In doing this we behold that image and become cursed ourselves. We lose the ability to be upright and partake of the glory of God.

We then have no true capability of maintaining face-to-face relationships with others, let alone with God. Our faces can only look into the eyes of others if our backs are upright. To be in a bowed-down position is to be hypnotized by the alluring and deceptive gaze of the poisonous serpent, an adversary both to God and the Church.

It has always been the desire and purpose of God to fully recover His image of glory in man. Moses' ministry prefigures the One Who would come as the very image of the glory in fullness (Hebrews 1:1) and transmit that anointing to His sons and daughters. The very image of God would oversee the construction of the structure called the Church, until it is completed and filled with glory. (Matthew 16:18.)

Moses was the shadow of Christ in that he prefigured the mediatorial work of Christ. Jesus the Christ indeed is responsible for raising up the true temple-house of glory. (John 2:19.) He is the One destined to bring the garments of righteousness with which to clothe the priesthood in His image and glory. (Luke 24:49; Acts 2:1-4; 2 Corinthians 3:18; John 14:3, 20:21.)

The building of the house and the mediation of the image are part and parcel of the Mosaic model of prophetic anointing. Moses had the power to mediate the image and communicate the Spirit by the bestowal of the Spirit on Joshua. (Numbers 27:20.) When Moses bestowed the Spirit on Joshua, the command of the Lord actually reads this way in the original: "You shall bestow your *majesty* on Joshua."

The word for "majesty" in the verse is *hod* in the Hebrew. The *hod* was the robe of glory with which a king was invested when he came to the throne.[2] In essence, Moses put his vestments of glory on Joshua, so that the same Spirit on and with him would be with Joshua. Thereby the people would obey Joshua even as they obeyed Moses, because the glory was now evident on him.

Prophetic Ministry Is One of Impartation

In the Mosaic economy, Joshua was commissioned to the prophetic office and vested with the same glory image. The picture is clearly one of a father investing his image in his son and offering him what is called the "double portion," or the right of the firstborn. (Deuteronomy 21:17.)

Moses invested himself in Joshua and reproduced his image in him, even as Seth was begotten in the image of

Adam. (Genesis 5:1-3.) This mediation by Moses is indeed a creative act of God, and yet transmitted by human agency. Prophetic ministry is often one of impartation. It is a calling forth of the potential invested in someone by God and transmitting to that person the ability to become that which they now have the power to be.

While this is an act of God in creative demonstration, it too is done through human agency. The New Covenant is a ministry of the Spirit according to Paul (2 Corinthians 3:1-12), and there is a transmission of the Spirit by human agency, inadequate as we are, into the lives of others. It is done both by prayer and *speech*.

In actual fact, the presence of the Spirit in the Church *is* the glory of God! As such, when prophets open their mouths to speak, there is authority and boldness in their words. Also, there is an activation of faith that overcomes whatever opposition would challenge the supremacy of Christ in daily life.

The creative fiat of God finds expression in us as His image is revealed in us and through us. The purpose of prophetic anointing in the aspect of building the Church is tied to opening the eyes and the awareness of the saints to the One Who indwells the Body of Christ.

The issue of "Christ in you" is the very *hope* of glory. The prophetic passion is for the glory of the Lord. The weighty and powerful presence of the Lord of glory in the midst of His people, indwelling the saints, is what prophetic faith cries to see released. There is a passionate conviction amongst those who are prophetically tempered and motivated to see God's intention realized in His people.

Those who have been awakened by the glory desire to be His agents of mediation for that glory in Christ. The six-winged creatures in Isaiah's vision cried out for a fullness of glory to fill the earth. (Isaiah 6:1-6.) Isaiah was overwhelmed and undone.

He longed to be a part of an earthly company that would help fill the earth with glory by passionate words of burning conviction, as the fiery seraphim spoke out of their internal fire and filled the heavenly temple with smoke. For Isaiah, for Moses, and for the Church, there is for us as bearers of the image of the Council an opportunity to be set on fire by the One Who came to baptize us in fire and give us the "spirit of burning."[3] (Isaiah 4:4; Matthew 3:11.)

The baptism of fire has a great deal to do with *passionate conviction and public demonstration.* When the fiery winged creatures cried out with intensity about the Holy One and His glory, the temple filled with the smoke of burning incense. The question we need to ask is: What was the origin of the incense?

This was not the altar where the coals were burning, this typified the altar where the crushed spices were burning and where the high priest would carry some in a censer into the Holy of Holies. This is from the Mosaic pattern of ascending glory.[4] (Exodus 30:1-10; Hebrews 9:4.) The closer one gets to the glory enthronement, the more fire is manifest.

Prophetic types are fiery types, passionate types, because they endeavor to live in close proximity to the glory! Even the lad Samuel lay down by the Ark of God. There was yet enough fire in the lampstand in the holy place for him to see where he was in relation to the purpose of God. (1 Samuel 3.)

The seraphims, like the cherubims, live closest to the throne and are ever ablaze with the glory of the Lord. As their cries released the burning incense *within* them, so our cries ought to be such that the places where we stand are filled with the smoke of God's glory! This cannot happen apart from a baptism of fire, a baptism of passion in the heart of the New Covenant community.

The prophetic voices in the Church often and ever are speaking of God's glory in a fiery and passionate manner.

As fire is all-consuming, so to them, God is an all-consuming fire, and His word in them is as fire shut up in their bones. (Jeremiah 20:9.)

The loss of fire is the cause for the lack of glory. The cause for the loss of fire is again tied to the *voices of the prophets*. (Acts 13:27.)

Pentecost Brought the Fire to Stay

In the encounter between Cleopas, a companion, and the risen Christ on the road to Emmaus, the Savior stepped into their conversation and endeavored to help them process their pain. (Luke 24:13.) They were *prevented*, however, from recognizing Him (Luke 24:16) and so treated Him as a stranger.

In the course of their revealing the struggle and confusion of their hearts, He finally called them foolish and *"slow of heart."* (Luke 24:25.) (If your heart beats too slowly, you probably are close to death, and your blood will run cold!)

The key to their "blindness," according to the Master, was that they had not believed all the *prophets had spoken*, at which point, Jesus began with Moses' prophetic utterances and took them on a course through the scriptures. He progressively opened up areas of insight until their hearts caught fire. (Luke 24:32.)

Once on fire, in a short period of time, they *ran* back to Jerusalem on the same road it had taken them all day to travel down. They returned to the upper room to relate their *experience*. They now had something burning in them. (Luke 24:33.)

They were incense bearers in the more perfect tabernacle being built by God, of which the Mosaic tabernacle was a type and a shadow. Upon the retelling of their experience, the upper room was filled with the incense of their burning hearts (their *passionate conviction* based on a living vision). They could make a *public declaration*, which the Lord of glory Himself bore witness to by appearing in their midst as they told the story! (Luke 24:36.)

The power of the story is compelling and appropriate for our understanding of the prophetic authority invested in the New Covenant community. Their passion, their fire, released in the telling of the story, enabled Him to stand in their midst and confirm their word with an infallible proof. (Luke 24:36; Acts 1:1,2.)

They were now adequate ministers of the New Covenant and of the Spirit. Their passionate conviction led them to use great boldness in their speech. Unlike Moses, they did not need to veil the glory of the image upon them, but released the glory so that the image could be seen! (2 Corinthians 3:12,13.)

The full significance of prophetic glory and power became evident in the fire that came to abide on the Day of Pentecost. The forty-day period of transition was preparatory for the Church, as it is was then to be fully invested with the glory image that the Mosaic pattern prefigured.

11

The Manifestation and Operation of Power

1. Through the process of being trained into our culture, we are taught to see as the other members of our society see. 2. We are strongly indoctrinated long before we seek to make any of our own choices in perceiving. 3. "Seeing" is interpreting (not simply observing). 4. Seeing is selective. 5. We see through "lenses" or "filters."[1]

— Dr. Charles Kraft

During the forty-day transitional period between Passover/Firstfruits and Pentecost, Jesus presented Himself among His followers. He walked with them and sat at meals with them, as had been His custom previously, explaining issues regarding Kingdom life and dynamics. (Acts 1:1-4.)

In the course of His conversations, He advised them to wait with focused attention in the upper room until God invested them with robes of authority.

On the Day of Pentecost, fifty days from the Feast of Firstfruits (which was on Resurrection Sunday that year), the priest was to bring new grain offering unto the Lord. The new grain offering was to be made of two loaves to be waved before the Lord (Leviticus 23:15-21), and in this offering, God would allow leaven. The offerings of bread at Pentecost are the only ones to which God allowed leaven to be added.

Passover involved an offering of unleavened bread, depicting symbolically the total "evenness" of Christ without additives in His sinless character and purity. However, the leaven in the two loaves of the Pentecost offering symbolizes the Body of Christ. The Body is made up of "Jew and Gentile" (all races — Ephesians 2:14-18), redeemed yet still imperfect, now pardoned by the sacrifice of Christ (represented in the offering of a sin offering).

These two, Jew and Gentile, are made one in Christ, and the middle wall of partition has come down. (Ephesians 2:14.) There is no "court of the Gentiles" in the New Temple. All are called to stand together before the Lord of glory!

It is worthy of note that the sons of Israel saw the glory of the Lord on Mount Sinai and received the Law exactly fifty days after the exodus. In terms of types and shadows, Pentecost therefore always has been associated with the reviving of God's people. On the Day of Pentecost, there was a renewal of the *ecclesia* and its desire to obey the Lord and fulfill His commissioning!

It is evident that at 9 a.m., the time of the wave and sin offering, there came a noise of turbulence, reminiscent of the sound of glory hovering over primeval chaos.[2] There was a rushing in of the wind of God. The picture of this was prefigured at Sinai:

> **And it came to pass on the third day in the morning, that there were thunders and lightnings, and a thick cloud upon the mount, and the voice of the trumpet exceeding loud; so that all the people that was in the camp trembled.**
>
> **Exodus 19:16**

The theophanic glory storm announced the arrival of God on Mount Sinai with the heavenly Council and all the attendants around the throne. There was also the blast of a trumpet giving clear awareness of the voice of the Lord being ready to be heard. (Also, see Hebrews 12:19-21.)

The account continues in intensity:

> And mount Sinai was altogether on a smoke, because the Lord *descended* upon it in fire: and the smoke thereof *ascended* as the smoke of a furnace, and the whole mount quaked greatly.
>
> And when the voice of the trumpet sounded long, and waxed louder and louder, Moses spake, and God answered him by a voice.
>
> And the Lord came down upon mount Sinai, on the top of the mount: and the Lord called Moses up to the top of the mount; and Moses went up.
>
> Exodus 19:18-20

Here in graphic and vivid detail are all the essential elements of Pentecost from a heavenly perspective. There first was the approach of the glory cloud as a storm cloud with violent wind and electricity. The arrival of the cloud was announced by thunder, lightning, and shaking. The tornado-like winds rocked the mountain effortlessly.

Then followed the blast of a trumpet which grew louder as the scene unfolded. In the process, out of the glory cloud / storm cloud there was a descending of the Lord on the mountain in the form of fire. This was followed by the ascension of smoke from the same mountain, and once again, the increase of the sound of the trumpet until Moses cried out in response and God answered him with thunder.

Pentecost Is Our Identification With Ascension

While Passover is our identity with resurrection, Pentecost is our identity with ascension.

Ascension ultimately provides access to stand in the heavenly Council. (See chapter 6: The Council of Jehovah.) As at Sinai, so in the New Covenant community on the Day of Pentecost, there was a tornado-like wind, an approaching glory storm of heavenly proportions, with a violent side to it that was heard as noise which filled the house. (Acts 2:1-11.)

This was followed by a shaking in the very physical arena. Then there was a descending of the Lord in the form of fire on the heads of the prepared disciples, followed by smoke rising back to God in the form of creative praise in many languages. This was a powerful demonstration of the presence of the living Christ in the midst of the company.

The voices of praise that declared the wonderful works of God supernaturally in other languages was as the *trumpet of God* to call His nation to His new mountain. This new mountain is called Zion, and it is made not of granite and quartz, but of "living stones" (1 Peter 2:4,5) created to give Him the glory due His name. (Hebrews 12:22-24.)

It was in this atmosphere of empowerment, being invested with the image of glory, the double portion, the right of the firstborn, that Peter stood in a boldness totally new to him. He began to open up Joel 2:28-32 with an authority and comprehension he never had before. He was now speaking as one *authorized*.

How was it possible for a braggart and a "wimp" to become a bold man of God in such a short period of time? It was possible because he had been vested in the image of glory and ascended into the Council. He was transformed into a prophetic mouthpiece for the One on the throne.

Peter had been granted *sanctuary privilege*, along with the rest of that company. We have dealt at length with the issue of sanctuary privilege and the concept of the prophet as the friend of God, as it occurs in the Old Testament. (See chapter 6.) What we now finally need to appreciate, in light of the significance of Pentecost, are the words of Jesus when He declared:

> This is my commandment, That ye love one another, as I have loved you.
>
> Greater love hath no man than this, that a man lay down his life for his friends.
>
> Ye are my friends, if ye do whatsoever I command you.

> Henceforth I call you not *servants*; for the servant knoweth not what his lord doeth: but I have called you *friends*; for all things that I have heard of my Father I have made known unto you.
>
> John 15:12-15

The company that had remained in the upper room until the Day of Pentecost was given the first taste of *sanctuary privilege*. In the process of the Feast of Firstfruits being fulfilled in Christ and His Church, the heavenly Council expanded its board of directors!

The exalted Christ had received from His Father the glory which He had originally. In turn, He passed on His anointing to all who believe. He began to pour out His Spirit, His image, His glory vestments, on all flesh for the purpose of prophetic directive and creative power.

There in Jerusalem, the Church began to touch every nation represented from around the known world. All the families of the earth were being blessed by the sons of the prophets who ministered His Spirit to those gathered that day. (Acts 3:25,26.)

So powerful was the manifestation and operation of this power that, when Peter lifted his voice like a trumpet, 3,000 new members were ushered into relationship in the glory cloud by the same wind that announced revival. (Acts 2:41.) Those added were offered sanctuary privilege without having to wait. The promise of the Father, long-awaited and now given, is available to all who call upon Him in Spirit and in truth.

Pentecost Restored Divine Order to the "Temple"

The coming of the glory Spirit on the Day of Pentecost was to alter the order of worship. There was an order yet taking place in the former temple, although the finished work of Christ caused God the Father to commission the flaming sword (Genesis 3:24) which guarded the way of access to the Tree of Life to cut the veil of separation and grant the nations free access.

This fulfillment had been the envy of all the Old Testament prophets. (John 8:56; Hebrews 11.) They knew a day was coming when all would have access into the Council. The arrival of the Spirit on the Day of Pentecost was for the purpose of divine order.

The Spirit knows the full mind and purpose of God. (1 Corinthians 2:11-13.) In His coming on the Day of Pentecost, He began the task of working with the saints to see the ultimate intention of God realized.[3] Pentecost announced the arrival of a new Leader (King, Savior, High Priest). Jesus was responsible for revealing the eternal purpose of God from eternity past to the Church, that the Church might in turn manifest it to the world.

T. A. Sparks made an insightful comment regarding this issue:

> There are many classifications into which men and women may be divided — as upper, middle or lower class; rich, well-to-do and poor; religious, skeptical and atheist . . . . But, as I think, the only categorization which really matters is that which divides men between the servants of the Spirit and the prisoners of the organization. That classification, which cuts right across all other classifications, is indeed the fundamental one. The idea, the inspiration, originates in the internal world, the world of the Spirit, and the idea having embodied itself in the organization, the organization then proceeds gradually to slay the idea which gave it birth.[4]

Peter's address and exegesis of the prophecy of Joel addressed racial, gender and class issues, and brought an understanding of divine empowerment to those who had ears to hear. The Spirit of the Lord had now come to administrate the affairs of the new Temple.

In the process, there was in that early beginning great persecution from the old, existing order. The Church had to be progressively and gradually untangled from the influences of legalism and mono-cultural norms. This "new thing," of which all the prophets spoke, had (and has) no interest in exclusivism, sectarianism, or denominationalism.

Peter stood before the multitude caught up in that mighty rushing wind and spoke as one with a prophetic directive, having an "understanding of the times, with knowledge of what Israel should do." (1 Chronicles 12:32.)

The prophetic significance of Peter's Pentecostal preaching has a great deal to do with the issue of recovery. For those of us in Western society at the end of the 20th century, it would behoove us to compare the Church to the model of the testimony of Jesus in the book of Acts.

The adored and honored Jerusalem had become a place of idolatry and corruption. The glory finally departed on the afternoon of the Passover when the Son of God cried out, **It is finished** (John 19:30). Persecution, however, had only just begun, as the Spirit working in the order of newness provided those who hungered and thirsted for righteousness the power to become sons and daughters of God.

He revealed to them that the finished work of Christ was the exit door from the trappings of the law. The blood of the Lamb paid the price for the indwelling principle of sin once and for all. From then on a higher law has been in operation, **the law of the Spirit of life in Christ Jesus** (Romans 8:2).

Those who believe have an authority over sin and can have rulership over their own unchecked passions and drives. (Galatians 5:24,25.) The law is no longer an external restriction, but a living and internal principle that can transform one's existence with an abundance of life. (Jeremiah 31:33; John 10:10; Hebrews 10:16.)

There are all too many places in, and areas of, the modern Church in which the prophetic paradigm of Pentecost has lost its impact. The Church has become enculturated into society, at least in America. It has conformed to the cosmos, the *arranged order of things*, and has failed to be made new again by the power of the Spirit, Who is the Lord.[5] (Romans 12:1,2; 2 Corinthians 3:17.)

If the Spirit is not Lord, there is no liberty. In fact, there is bondage. The issue is quite evident: no Lordship, no liberty! There cannot be true freedom apart from the government of God's Spirit in our lives.

Conformity has always been the danger for the Church in the world and the focus of much prophetic input. John the apostle reminds us that if any man loves the *present, systematized, arranged order of things*, the passionate, fiery, and fervent love of the Father is not in him. (1 John 2:15.)

For those who embrace the Word of God, just as it was for Paul, there ought be a desire for the faith of those we touch to rest on God, manifest in the demonstration of His Spirit and His power. (1 Corinthians 2:4,5.)

For the Church to be transformed, it must have a renewal in its perception of reality. The mind of God must become the mind of the Church. Renewal is essential to transformation, which is the *transcending* of a form or structure no longer capable of housing the new thing the Father desires to accomplish.

The Church cannot be a prophetic community in the manifestation and operation of the dynamic of God's Spirit without acknowledging and repenting of false concepts of perception. We must deal with false fields of knowledge that have dominated us consciously and unconsciously.

The domination of our thought processes (which is conformity to the world) is part of this issue of enculturation. Our thinking can be dominated by secularism when it is held captive to idolatrous beliefs and the *reasonings and speculations* of the prevailing culture. (2 Corinthians 10:5.)

The Church Must Become Un-Culterated

"Culture" comes from the Latin *cultus*, which implies a body of people embracing a set of beliefs. In essence, this is a form of worship which, apart from the knowledge of God, is *idolatry*. What we need to comprehend is that the power of idolatry is the power of *words!*

The effective use of language in rhetoric, metaphor, and oratory can hypnotize us[6] and cause us to lose any sense of continuity with our destiny, or our history as the people of God. To be numbed to our history and blinded to our destiny is to be locked into the emptiness of hopeless existence.

Prophetic ministry strongly reacts to the dehumanizing effect of the "words of whisperers," which penetrate the unconscious realms of man's mind and subversively tamper with territories of mind and spirit that are the exclusive property of God Himself. (Proverbs 18:8.)

A society that thrives, as does modern society, on rhetoric has the ability to manipulate a people through word power. This manipulation enculturates (or "programs") a set of presumptions into its hearers that causes them never to think about their heritage or their destiny in God.

Godlesssness is typical today of society in general. The powers and principalities have systematized evil so that it has saturated all forms of education. There is now an ingrown predisposition to unbelief from a very tender age.

In order for an idolatrous society to survive, it must of necessity blind the masses to anything but the present moment. They must ever and always be tyrannized by what is urgent in their present moment.

We live in a day when the prophetic voice needs to urgently speak to the issues that have robbed the souls of humanity from history and destiny. The belief that prevails and mocks is universally present and manifests in a philosophy of "what is happening right now is what is important."

The eternal God stands diametrically opposed to such falsehood. The eternal One is intent on forming and fashioning people through history, destiny, and present adversity to righteously model what true *community* is like.

The adversity the people of God endure is due to the resistance they offer to the powers and principalities, by rejecting false notions and idolatrous concepts. They are sojourners, like Abraham, looking for the city which has foundations whose builder and maker is God. (Hebrews 11:10.)

Peter's discourse on the Day of Pentecost promised a prophetic flow, from the elder statesmen in the government of God to the servants and children in every sphere of community life.[7] This prophetic flow could overcome the rhetoric of the false empires of secularism and triumph over them by the power of prophetic speech.

Prophetic speech delivered poetically reshapes perceptions and realities and challenges false imaginations. It can reclaim the imagination for God and God alone! The lens of prophetic language and imagery is poetic for a specific reason. The word *poetry* comes from the Greek word *poieo*, which means "to fashion and shape, or creatively make."

Poetry is creative speech designed to lift the imagination to a realm of intuiting the real, though unseen, world of God. It can cause the lofty and high things of false images to be demolished in the minds and hearts of men and women. God has not built His Kingdom on rhetoric, but on passionate, powerful prophetic speech. (1 Corinthians 2:1-16.)

The "persuasive words of men's wisdom" is the rhetoric of manipulation, control, and enculturation. Prophetic speech has in it the demonstrative life of the Spirit and the power to transform the hearer until the hearer can "see" and "hear" the Word, destiny, and purpose of God in his or her life.

The Church needs prophetic ministry and speech, because such ministry is rooted in the heart of the Father. Prophetic speech is replete with the memory of where we have come from and the hope of where we shall yet arrive. It causes the present moment to be pregnant with possibility and potential that refuses to settle for "whatever is essential is what is happening now."

Prophetic speech, as it was delivered on the Day of Pentecost, provided the community of the hopeful with a way to accurately define their current reality in light of a promise made centuries before. It spoke forth a destiny that would excel centuries after.

For indeed, the promise was for those who heard it when Peter spoke, but also for those who would hear it generations afterward. The promise had the power to transform the past, present and the future. Joel, the poet-prophet who endured a plague of devastation in his own reality, turned his gaze towards the unseen arena. There in the presence of Jehovah, the lens of his imagination was corrected to see that his present circumstance was taking place for a future object lesson.

It catapulted him into a future that touched not only the company in the upper room, or the 3,000 ushered into the Kingdom by his poetic speech, but his prophetic imagination has been used by the Spirit to touch following generations. Peter prophetically waxed eloquent, saying it in this fashion:

> **For the promise is unto you, and to your children, and to all that are afar off, even as many as the Lord our God shall call.**
>
> **Acts 2:39**

The speech that provided an architectural framework for the restructuring of the imagination of the community of the redeemed was energized by the memory of God in ages past. That "memory" (given us by the Word of God) provides a reference point for our origins, then radically renews our hope for the future. It calls things that are not as though they are, enabling us in the present reality of things not to succumb to the pressure of "eat, drink, and be merry, for tomorrow we die." (Luke 12:19,20.)

Unlike the world, we are not evolving, but rather we are *transforming* our current reality in order to stretch us to contain God's ultimate objective: the fullness of His glory, in Christ, in His Church. (Ephesians 4:13.)

12

The Call to the Future

Most people know the future only as a place
that is always robbing them of their security,
breaking promises, changing the rules on them,
causing them all sorts of troubles. And yet, it is in
the future where our greatest leverage is.[1]

— Joel Arthur Barker

Futurist Joel Arthur Barker got the attention of the
corporate world in the early 90s with his concepts about
anticipating the future. He continued.

We can't change the past, although if we are
smart, we learn from it. Things happen only in one
place — the present. And usually we react to those
events. The "space" of time in the present is too
slim to allow for much more. It is the yet-to-be
future, and only there, where we have the time to
prepare for the present.[2]

Another "futurist," who spoke more than 2,500 years
ago, made the following statement that puts a "living edge"
on Barker's insight:

**For I know the thoughts that I think toward you,
saith the Lord, thoughts of peace, and not of evil, to
give you an expected end.**

Jeremiah 29:11

The English translation, *an expected end*, literally says,
"a hope and a future." God's plans for the Israelites were

117

for good, not for evil. Jeremiah gave that Word in a context of exile and deportation. The people of God, who had spent centuries anticipating the land of promise and finally arrived, were being exiled from the land. They were having to deal with the loss of the promise due to their failure to put God in remembrance.

Idolatry robbed them of their relationship with the One Who transcends time and space, and works all things after the counsel of His Will, and thus they cut off their hope for the future. However, in exile, those who heeded the voice of the prophet and lived by the words he uttered were able to live in anticipation of a promised future. That remnant was able not merely to cope with the present situation, but to make the most of it.

The Old Covenant prophet was in many ways different from the New Covenant prophet, yet also similar. The manner in which both eras of prophets approach life is tied to their passion for God and His purpose. Jeremiah gives us an understanding of how the prophetic word works in the one delivering it and in those receiving it to shape the future in cooperation with God.

The articulation and declaration of the heart of God requires a deep and abiding trust and intimacy between the Commissioner and the one commissioned. God as Mentor is a pattern we must learn to discern in our spiritual journey towards His full thought. If God is Mentor, we are His students in training to partake of His fullness received in Christ. (John 1:16.)

Our journey towards wholeness is fraught with danger, possibility, and amazement. In considering the call to the future, it will be beneficial to consider the role of the prophetic in preparing the Church for the future. Given the nature and purpose of the ascension-gift ministries listed in Ephesians, we realize the "gifts" together are to serve one unifying purpose: for all believers to attain to the ultimate desire and thought of the Father. (Ephesians 4:11-17.)

In the process of seeing the Church become what God called it to be, we discover that all the ministry gifts are given for *equipping*. (Ephesians 4:12.) The Greek word Paul used, translated "equipping," is a medical technical term for the "setting of a bone." The noun form of the Greek word describes the dynamic act by which persons or things are properly conditioned.[3]

To Be "Equipped" Means To Be Restored

The picture shown us by that word is that equipping is actually a healing and restoring process. For a bone to need to be set implies that it has been broken or fractured. The same word was translated in Galatians 6:1 as "restore." In essence, Paul equated the ascension-gift ministries with the process of restoration.

Sin had its crippling effect on all humanity, and once Christ is embraced by those aware of their brokenness, the Spirit desires to begin a restoring work in their lives. Restoration is at the heart of prophetic ministry and at the very heart of God.

All gift ministries are set in the Body for the purpose of "setting the bones." For a bone to be set, there must be a relationship — a joint (or "joining point"), if you will — between the broken bone and the bones closest to the break. The design of prophetic ministry is for the purpose of making connections between the visible and the invisible.

In the vision of the valley of dry bones, Ezekiel was commanded to prophesy to the bones, until by the power of God, the bones came together, bone to its bone. (Ezekiel 37:7.) The heart of God is for His people to come together. This cannot happen without the powerful intervention of the Spirit covering us in brooding fashion to bring order out of the chaotic pile of "dead men's bones."

It is the purpose of the prophetic voice to impart, then "feed and water" the awareness of a state of being, life that is redemptive. It is to pull us into the future before the future has arrived. Prophetic ministry and imagination are designed by God to be the catalyst that expands and stretches our awareness of who He is, where He has come from, and where He is going.

In discovering who He is, where He has come from, and where He is going, our definition of *who we are* must be redefined. We cannot know who we are, since we are made in His image, if we do not know Him. The prophetic imagination helps us by nourishing in us a new perspective through the power of expansive speech. Words that touch our untapped creativity and potential call forth out of us something we have never quite been able to articulate but have always "sensed" was true.

The prophetic perspective does not rise out of anything that already is, but is based on an encounter with a form and substance of reality that is *yet to be.* Energized by the divine imagination, prophets challenge the constructs of reality and call "things that are not as though they are," in the true tradition of Abraham, the father of the faith. (Romans 4:17.)

The architectural framework of prophetic imagination is found in the dream-room of God Himself. When some believe the sky is falling, prophets discern a crack in the egg-shell of limited existence. Others tremble in fear, believing their world is falling apart. Prophets rejoice that old orders are ending, for they are too limited to give expression to the life they carry.

Unless the shell of the wheat cracks (dies), the plant cannot grow up out of the ground. (John 12:24.) The principle of death is the cracking of the shell to let the larger life within the shell find its own unique expression. If the sky is falling, it is only the *old* sky. The prophet then begins to look for the "new heavens and new earth" (Isaiah 66:22), with a much larger capacity to contain the dream held in God's heart from ages past.

Jesus as prophet was nothing less than revolutionary. He was the reality of which Jeremiah was a shadow. He was set over the nations to "pluck up, break down, destroy, overthrow, build, and plant." (Jeremiah 1:10.) This is revolutionary indeed. A *revolution* is "a forcible overthrow of an established government or political system."[4] It is a completely pervasive, usually radical, change in something that often happens rather quickly.

Jesus saw the potential of a nation being born in a day, once the powers of darkness were overthrown. (Isaiah 66:8.) The most revolutionary act in all of history was the crucifixion of the Son of God. It was there that He totally disarmed principalities and powers and "made a spectacle of them openly, triumphing over them" through the act of death. (Colossians 2:15.)

He overcame limitation by allowing it to attempt to limit Him. Yet how can the finite contain or limit the infinite? All death did was crack the eggshell of Jesus' humanity. The divine nature stared death in the face and swallowed it up in absolute victory. Jesus "gave birth" in one moment to a holy nation of priests who came forth out of His side from which flowed both blood and water! (John 19:34.)

For this reason, the prophets moved and still move in a parameter beyond predictability. The prophetic unction is both constant and variable at the same time. It is the very nature of God to be known and unknown, knowable and beyond comprehension. The prophet lives in that blessed paradox and finds much food for contemplation in the presence of Him whose glory consumes him or her.

We Must Have a Word To Go Before Us

The future is subject to His dream and therefore is open-ended. Those "addicted" to predictability will seek to limit His free agency and constrain Him to meet them on more secure levels of logic and reason. But those who are hungering and thirsting for the dream of God, the passion and pathos of the Godhead, will hear the "fresh word" from His throne.

Sermonizing is for lecturers and pulpiteers, the prophet needs a *word*! It must be a "proceeding" word (i.e., "from the mouth of God," Deuteronomy 8:3) going ahead of them into the future, revealing the intention before it arrives, so that the present becomes pregnant with new meaning and relevance.

The prophetic motivation and imagination is built by God on the sure awareness that His creative word can alter the epochs of history and restructure reality until it fulfills His purpose. (Hebrews 11:3.) The prophet will see more in the invisible than others see in the visible.

When Elisha and many of the nation of Israel were besieged in Samaria, surrounded by chariots and horsemen ready to take their lives, his servant was full of anxiety and fear. (2 Kings 6:16,17.) In this seemingly perilous situation, Elisha only asked God for one thing: He asked that the servant be allowed to see what he already saw with the eyes of his spirit.

What the servant "saw" was chariots and horses of fire that more than outnumbered the Arameans. The constructs of mind and reality in which the Arameans and the servant lived were such that they were blinded to the greater reality of which Elisha was continually aware.

There has always been and always will be a delicate balance in handling the canon of Scripture between the Law and the Prophets. Our ability to anticipate the future requires we maintain that balance. In its widest application, the Law itself is prophetic. The types and shadows contained in the Pentateuch all pointed to the reign of Christ in some shape or fashion.

It is evident from Peter's vision of the four-cornered sheet with all the unclean animals of earth and air, that God was not ultimately concerned with whether Peter ate pork, or rattlesnake, or carrion. (Acts 10:11-16.) In some way, the stipulations of the Law concerning food were merely a prophetic indication of the nations to be brought into "cleanness" in the future harvest to begin with Jesus.

The differentiation between "clean" and "unclean" in the Law had to do with proximity to the Holy of Holies. Now that Christ had come, He had brought and proclaimed *shalom* (peace) to those who were near, and *shalom* to those who were far from the sanctuary. (Isaiah 57:19; Ephesians 2:17.) Neither those near or far had sanctuary privileges at that time, except through the high priest once a year and the true prophets of Jehovah.

However, in Christ's finished work, all nations are declared clean and have prophetic-priestly privilege to hear the secrets of God and His dreams for the future. Then peoples from all tribes and nations can shout from the housetops the determined will of God and our hope for a great and glorious future to break in upon us.

The community that dealt with the Law of Moses from a place of rigidity became short-sighted, with no discernment about the future. They only have an expectation of judgment on those that do not fit *their* image of God. Short-sightedness makes us "deaf" to the fact that God is free to do as He wills!

There is a tendency when dealing with the Law to do what Israel did: cause it to be carried out to the letter. Paul told us, however, that the letter kills, but the Spirit makes alive. (2 Corinthians 3:6.) Those who live by the letter have a need for everything to be known and manageable, but the life of God moves beyond the borders of human management. Prophetic ministry does not deal with the "letter" as it is known. It recognizes that the life of the Spirit carries the element of surprise and amazement.

The prophetically motivated individual or community will often raise more questions than they answer, because they are immersed in the power of God's creative expression. It is not that the prophet challenges the law, but rather the prevailing belief of those who have used the law to manipulate and coerce others to do things their way.

True prophetic ministry always seems to call into question the status quo. It is sometimes so radical in nature that the status quo will call the prophetic anything but God! The religious establishment called Jesus a "blasphemer" (Matthew 9:3) and "Beelzebub." (Matthew 10:25.)

Paul was given the privilege of being called a "heretic." (Acts 24:14.) Both Jesus and Paul were judged as having "laid aside" the Law of Moses. (John 7:19-24; Acts 21:28.) In spite of the accusations and the persecution, both declared that what they did and what they preached was the fulfillment of the Law.

The integrity of true prophetic ministry requires that there be an identification with the message preached. *The prophet is the message.* Someone once said, "a living prophet is different from an academic one"!

Prophetic ministry still has a future.

There is yet a glory into which the Church must be called.

There is yet the full thought and intention of God to be realized in the earth.

There is yet a need to call the people of God to rise out of mediocrity into the greatness of God's glory with a passion for His presence.

While it is the tendency for all of us to live in comfort zones of our own making, the prophet will always come into that territory to *pluck up, break down, destroy, and overthrow* before he or she can build and plant! The breakthrough of fresh illumination from the Word of truth is always surrounded by conflict.

For those with a sense of the glorious future in store for the Church of the living God, those who are prophetically tempered, motivated, gifted or called, the only consolation is the promise of God's abiding presence!

Be not afraid of their faces: for I am with thee to deliver thee, saith the Lord.

Jeremiah 1:8

Endnotes

Introduction

[1]Snyder, Howard A. *Earthcurrents, The Struggle for the World's Soul*, (Nashville: Abingdon Press, 1995), p. 17.

Chapter 1

[1]Long, Zeb Bradford and McMurry, Douglas. *The Collapse of the Brass Heaven* [a saga of the transformation of two evangelical pastors by the Holy Spirit-infilling], (Grand Rapids: Chosen Books, Baker Book House, 1994), p. 17.

[2]*Random House Dictionary of the English Language*, (New York: Random House, 1968).

[3]Brueggemann, Walter. *The Prophetic Imagination*, (Philadelphia: Fortress Press, 1978). Brueggemann's profound and timely statement is his application of the insights of Peter Berger and Thomas Luckmann in *The Social Construction of Reality*, (New York: Doubleday Books, 1967).

Chapter 2

[1]Kline, Meredith. *Images of the Spirit*, (Grand Rapids: Baker Book House, 1980).

[2]*Ibid.*

[3]Bright, John. *The Kingdom of God*, (Nashville: Abingdon Press, 1953). p. 89. (Over the years and after much studying of Scripture and verb forms, I have come to believe that indeed something occurred (possibly Satan's fall from heaven) that caused a perfect earth to become "null and void," meaning there is a gap in time between verses 1 and 2 of Genesis 1. I refer the reader to *Without Form and Void* by Canadian professor, theologian, and

author, Dr. Arthur C. Custance, (Ontario: Doorway Publications, 1970), perhaps the most definitive work I have found on this subject, dealing with the text from the Hebrew, the Latin Vulgate, the Septuagint, and finally, the English.)

[4] Kline. *Op. Cit.*

[5] Land, George T. *Grow or Die, the Unifying Principle of Transformation*, 1973.

[6] Chironna, Mark J. *The Undiscovered Christ*, (Shippensburg, PA: Destiny Image, 1991.)

[7] Kline. *Op. Cit.*, p. 17.

[8] For a complete study of the pattern and types of the tabernacle, refer to the works of Ada Haberson, Kregel Publications, Grand Rapids, MI; C. W. Slemming, Christian Literature Crusade, Fort Washington, PA; and Andrew Jukes, also published by Kregel.

Chapter 3

[1] Morris, Henry M. *The Remarkable Record of Job*, (Grand Rapids: Baker Book House, 1988), pp. 86,87.

[2] Kline. *Op. Cit.*, pp. 16,17.

[3] Brueggemann. *Op. Cit.*, p. 13.

[4] *The Pulpit Commentary*, (Hendrickson); *Smith's Bible Dictionary*, (MacDonald Publishing Company).

[5] In popular Pentecostal and Charismatic teaching, the "spirit of prophecy" is considered an anointing for all to prophesy when there is a "canopy of glory" in a gathering. Then there is the "gift of prophecy" (1 Corinthians 12), in which only those so endowed can operate, and finally, the third and highest manifestation, the office of prophet. The principles are right, but this scripture is not one that applies. Its application in this doctrine means twisting the verse away from its connection with Jesus. I contend that we cannot reduce the biblical concept of the prophetic to an utterance or a word of knowledge. There is a greater frame of reference in which the prophetic is recognized in Holy Writ. The prophetic voice speaks to the nature and revelation of Christ in and with the Church and provides an architectural framework for steering the Church in God's intended direction.

[6] Sparks Tape Ministry.

Chapter 4

[1] Packer, J. L. *God's Words*, (Grand Rapids: reprinted by Baker Book House, 1988, copyright by Packer, 1981, first published by Inter-Varsity Press), p. 116.

[2] Wight, Fred H. *Manners and Customs of Bible Lands*, (Chicago: Moody Bible Institute, 1953), p. 290.

[3] For a detailed consideration of issues of kingship, see *The Land*, by Breuggemann, (Philadelphia: Fortress Press, 1977) in which he does a masterful job of articulating the purpose of kings in Israel.

[4] *Ibid.*

Chapter 5

[1] Jordan, James B. *Through New Eyes*, (Brentwood, TN: Wolgemuth & Hyatt, Publishers, Inc., 1988).

[2] Heschel, Abraham J. *The Prophets*, (New York: Harper Torchbooks, 1962), Vol. 2, p. xii.

[3] MacKay, Donald M., "Christian Priorities in Science," *Journal of the American Scientific Affiliation*, June, 1986; used in *Science and Religion* (San Diego: Greenhaven Press, Inc., 1988), p. 214.

[4] *Cruden's Complete Concordance*, (Gordonsville, TN: Dugan Publishers, Inc.), "Interpreting Dictionary."

[5] The actual translation of "planted by streams of living water" in Psalm 1 in the Hebrew is "transplanted trees by irrigation canals." The psalm was written during the time of the deportation into Babylon, where most of the water was brought by irrigation canals into the dry and arid land. The exiles saw themselves uprooted and expelled from the sanctuary. They found themselves by "rivers" where they could maintain ceremonial purity for the purpose of prayer and restoration. (See Ezekiel 1.)

[6] Jordan, *Op. Cit.*

Chapter 6

[1] Wood, Leon J. *The Prophets of Israel*, (Grand Rapids: Baker Book House, 1979, 1985), p. 16.

[2] Wood, *A Survey of Israel's History*, (Grand Rapids: Academic Books, Zondervan Publishing House, 1986), p. 299.

[3] Hanke, Howard A. *The Thompson Chain Reference Bible Survey*, (Waco: Word Books, copyright 1981 by B. B. Kirkbride Co.), p. 299.

[4] Kline, *Op. Cit.*

[5] *Cruden's Complete Concordance.*

[6] Genesis 18:22,23; Exodus 32:7-14; Numbers 16:20-24; and Amos 7:1-6.)

Chapter 7

[1] Bruce, F. F. *The Message of the New Testament*, (Exeter, England: The Paternoster Press, 1972, 1983), p. 26.

[2] Kline. *Op. Cit.*, p. 58.

[3] Peterson, Eugene. *The Message*, (Navpress.)

[4] *Maimonides: Guide to the Perplexed*, (Chicago: Chicago Press.)

[5] *Strong's Concordance*, "The Greek Dictionary of the New Testament," #5056, p. 71. Also, the careful student of Scripture may want to study *telos* in the works of Brown, Driver, Briggs and Harris, Archer, Waltke for the full impact of the Greek and the Hebrew from the account in Exodus as well as Paul's summing up in 2 Corinthians 3:7-11.

[6] In Revelation 1:10, "I was *becoming in the Spirit*," is a more literal translation. The Greek word is *ginomai*, meaning "to become."

[7] Note that in John 3:11, Jesus spoke in the plural on behalf of another and perhaps the rest of the heavenly Council in His use of "we." He was declaring that He is a participant in the divine Council. Then, He went on to confirm His having been "apostlized" in verse 17, when He said that the Son was *sent* (the English translation of the Greek word, *apostello*).

Chapter 8

[1] Coleman, William L. *The Pharisee's Guide to Total Holiness*, (Minneapolis: Bethany House Publishers, 1977), pp. 26,29,106,128.

[2] *Ibid*, p. 110.

[3] Elwell, Walter A., Gen. Ed. *Baker's Encyclopedia of the Bible*, (Grand Rapids: Baker Book House, 1988), Vol. 2, p. 1447; also, see the Introduction, p. xxiii of The Messiah Texts, by Raphael Patai, (Detroit: Wayne State University Press, copyright 1979 by Patai),

which gives in detail 3,000 years (up to the present) of Jewish "myths" and beliefs concerning the expected Messiah.

[4]Kline, *Kingdom Prologue,* (Gordon Conwell Seminary, 1986).

[5]Coleman. *Op. Cit.,* p. 123.

Chapter 9

[1]Calvin, John. *Institutes of the Christian Religion* III.xx.2.

[2]*The Best of E. M. Bounds on Prayer,* (Grand Rapids: Baker Book House, 1981), p. 99.

[3]*Ibid,* pp. 89,90.

[4]For a study showing that the plagues involved God showing the Egyptians their gods were useless, see *Moses and the Gods of Egypt,* by John J. Davis, (Grand Rapids: Baker Book House, 1991.)

[5]Peterson, *Reversed Thunder,* (New York: Harper Collins, 1988).

Chapter 10

[1]Hayford, Jack. *Worship His Majesty,* (Dallas: Word Publishing, 1987), p. 178.

[2]For further study of the word, see the following scriptures: 1 Chronicles 29:25; Psalm 45:3, 145:5.

[3]The seraphim, or literally, "burning one," has six wings. Six is the number for *man* in Scripture. In some way, therefore, the "burning one" reveals an image of God and His glory intended to inspire *man* to bear the same fire and manifest the same glory.

[4]Note that the word for "altar" in this passage also can be translated "censer," which is more accurate, as there was no other altar in the Holy of Holies than the Ark. The altar of incense was outside the veil. Yet, once a year, when the high priest entered within the veil, he brought with him the blood of sprinkling and a censer filled from the burning incense just outside the veil. This is a picture of pure spiritual worship and the fire of God within the hearts of the saints. In Revelation 5:8, we see that the angelic council carry "golden bowls" of incense into the immediate presence of God, and this "incense" is the prayers of the saints.

Chapter 11

[1] Kraft, Charles. *Christianity in Culture: A Study in Dynamic Biblical Theologizing in Cross-Cultural Perspective*, (Maryknoll, NY: Orbis Publishers, 1979), p. 53.

[2] The reader is encouraged to compare the sights and sounds of the glory cloud references in Genesis in the *Septuagint* Bible to the glory cloud in Acts, the English versions.

[3] I borrowed the phrase "ultimate intention" from a great man of God named DeVerne Fromke. His book, *God's Ultimate Intention*, published by Christian Literature Crusade, is still one of the best — if not the definitive work — on Paul's concept of God's wisdom hidden for generations, but now revealed.

[4] Sparks. *Op. Cit.*

[5] 2 Corinthians 3:17 actually reads, **Now the Lord *is* that Spirit: and where the Spirit of the Lord is, there is liberty.**

[6] When Paul addressed the church at Rome, he admonished them to "awaken from sleep." The Greek word translated "sleep" is *hupno*, from which we get "hypnotize," meaning "to put under." Idolatry "puts us under" prevailing beliefs that dominate our actions and cause us to behave in ways of which we are not consciously aware.

[7] A careful exegetical study of the Hebrew language of Joel 2:28 shows there is a clear recognition of divine government and of the flow of divine authority and anointing to the entire community by prophetic release.

Chapter 12

[1] Barker, Joel Arthur. *Future Edge*, (New York: William Morrow and Co., 1992).

[2] *Ibid.*

[3] Reinecker & Rogers. *Linguistic Key to the Greek New Testament*, (Grand Rapids: Zondervan Publishing House, 1976).

[4] *Random House Dictionary.*